THE PIKETON MURDERS

RUTH KANTON

TABLE OF CONTENTS
THE PIKETON MURDERS
STALKED & ABDUCTED
KELSIE SCHELLING
BRITTANEE DREXEL
MISTY COPSEY
RAILROAD KILLER
MISSING MADELEINE
BEAUMONT CHILDREN
PATRICIA MEEHAN
ARLIS PERRY

Pike County Shootings

The Rhoden family members have been residents in Pike County, Ohio, for generations. The family was well known in the small knit community, and was well regarded. Dana Lynn Rhoden met Christopher Rhoden Sr. in high school and the two fell in love at first sight. Family and friends described Chris as a hardworking and dedicated family man who was well regarded by those that knew him or dealt with him. Dana was a nurse, and friends described her as a gregarious character who was fun to be around and had an easy smile. The couple had three children together – Clarence "Frankie" Rhoden, Hannah May Rhoden, and Christopher Rhoden Jr. After 22 years of marriage, Chris and Dana divorced, but they remained close. To ensure that they remained close to their children, Chris bought Dana a house in the same property as his on Union Hill Road.

Their first born, 20-year-old Frankie, lived in the same area with his fiancée, Hannah Hazel Gilley, and their son. 19-year-old Hannah Hazel had finished high school and had plans of attending college and studying business. She wanted to open her own daycare someday. Frankie and Hannah Hazel were making plans of getting married soon, and were looking forward to having a big family. Frankie was described as a hardworking man who loved fishing, hunting, and the demolition Derby. Frankie was the father of two sons, 3-year-old

Brentley Rhoden – who he fathered with an ex – and 6-month-old Ruger Lee Rhoden. April 2006 was a special month for the family – Hannah May was about to give birth – and weeks earlier, Dana had thrown her a big baby shower. The photos showed that the family was having a great time, and that they were happy. Hannah May was mother to two daughters – 2-year-old Sophia and newborn Kylie. Hannah May lived with her mother, and shared custody of Sophia with her ex, Edward "Jake" Wagner. Also in the same house was 16-year-old Chris Jr., who was a freshman at a local high school.

Chris Sr. was always happy to help out anyone who needed him, and would often have his cousin – Gary Rhoden – staying with him.

April 22, 2016

Dana Rhoden's sister, Bobby Jo Manley, had been asked by Chris Sr. to feed his pets that morning because he and Gary wouldn't be around. With Hannah May having given birth to daughter Kylie just five days earlier, Chris Sr. knew that Dana would have her hands full taking of their daughter and granddaughter. Bobby Jo gladly agreed, and drove over to Chris Sr.'s house sometime past 7 a.m. on April 22, 2016. When she walked into the house, she was met by a gruesome sight. The house was bloody, and the bodies of the two men were covered in a great deal of blood. Bobby Jo immediately called the police, and her call was received at 7:51 a.m. by the dispatcher. A hysterical Bobby Jo tried describing the scene, and told the 911 operator that the two men looked like they had been badly beaten. Bobby Jo provided the house address, and the operator asked her to walk outside the house and stay there. She was also asked to make sure that no one else went into the house. The shaken Bobby Jo left the house and closed the door behind her.

Once outside the home, Bobby Jo decided to walk to Frankie's home and let him know what had happened to his father and uncle. She rushed to the house and knocked, after a few moments, Frankie's 3-year-old son, Brentley, opened the door. The first thing Bobby Jo noticed was that the little boy was covered in blood, and seemed uncharacteristically confused. She asked him where daddy was, and Brentley stated that daddy was playing zombie in the bedroom. Knowing that the family watched *The Walking Dead* frequently, Bobby Jo became alarmed. She picked up the little boy and headed towards the main bedroom of the house. She was greeted by yet another grisly scene. Frankie and his fiancée, Hannah Hazel, were lying dead in their bed, and it looked like they had both been shot in the head. Their 6-month-old son, Ruger Lee, was lying in the bed between his deceased parents. Bobby Jo, now in hysterics, called her brother, James Manley, and asked him to check on their sister and the other kids. James rushed over to Dana's home to make sure that they were okay.

When James got to his sister's house, he was greeted by an ugly scene. Dana was in her bedroom, shot in her face. He headed to Hannah May's room, and found his niece dead in her bed, with her five day old daughter in bed with her. He checked on the child, and thankfully, she was still alive. He searched for Chris Jr., but he was nowhere to be found. Police were called to the three homes, with reports of 6 dead, one missing teen, and three children left alive at the scene.

It didn't take long for the news of the murders to spread within the community. Police began arriving at the scene, and it didn't long for them to call for backup. As more and more officers arrived on Union Hill Road, residents began getting snippets of information about what had happened in the three homes. Ruger Lee, Brentley, and 5 day old Kylie were taken by Children Protective Services agents, as police unraveled what was going on. No one had seen or heard from Chris Jr. that day, and he was labeled as a missing person. Officers were dispatched to the high school he attended, but none of his friends reported hearing from him, and he hadn't shown up at school that day. Calls were made to relatives, but no one had seen the teenager or heard from him. The Pike County Sheriff's Office quickly called the Ohio Criminal Bureau of Investigation (CBI) and asked for help. The sheriff already understood that his department was not equipped to handle a case of such magnitude, not because his officers were incompetent – but because his office lacked the resources to handle the case.

About 7 hours after Bobby Jo first called 911, dispatchers received one more call, this time from a few miles away from the initial crime scene. At 1:26 p.m., Donald Stone, having seen the news about the murder of the Rhoden family members, decided to check up on his cousin, 44-year-old Kenneth Rhoden. Kenneth was

Chris Sr.'s older brother, and Stone had not heard from him that day. When he got to the house, Stone found Kenneth dead, with what appeared to be a gunshot wound in his face. He was covered with dollar bills strewn about his body. Officers were quickly dispatched to the scene, Kenneth being the seventh member of the Rhoden family found killed. Breaking news reports were frequent, and members of the community were glued to their screens, dumbfounded and shocked that something like this could happen in the small town.

With no clue about what happened to the family, investigators combed through the crime scenes. Hours after reporting Chris Jr. missing, he was finally located in his mother's house. He was found dead, with apparent gunshot wounds to the head. The investigators had everyone else in the family accounted for, and Chris Jr.'s body brought the finally tally of the deceased to eight. He was the youngest victim, and investigators were still confused about why the killer or killers murdered him but left the other minor in the house alive. In addition to the CBI, the Federal Bureau of Investigation also sent its agents to help in the investigation. With no apparent motive, investigators couldn't rule out the possibility that thrill seekers were responsible for the murders, and that they wouldn't strike again.

Autopsies

Once the initial crime scene analyses were complete, the bodies were taken to the Hamilton County Coroner's Office in Cincinnati. The final report concluded that all the victims had been shot, and a total of

32 bullet wounds were counted. All the victims were shot multiple times, except one. The Medical Examiner believed that Chris Sr. may have been awake when the killer or killers attacked him. He was shot a total of 9 times in the head and torso, and was the only victim who was shot anywhere else apart from the head. He had a gunshot wound through his right arm, which shattered his bones. Investigators theorized that this was most likely a defensive wound, and that he had raised his arm to protect himself. He was shot in the head, limbs, and torso, and one bullet went through his cheek. The examination also found wood fragments on his body, most likely gotten when he was dragged through the house. Gary Rhoden was shot twice in the head and once in the face. One of the shots to the side of the head had a muzzle stain, which showed that the killer had

been standing close to Gary when he pulled the trigger, and had pressed the gun hard against Gary's temple.

Frankie was shot 3 times in the head, and investigators believed that he and Hannah Hazel were dead asleep when the killer or killers made their way into the house. Hannah Hazel was shot 5 times in the head and face, and one bullet went through her left eye. Dana Rhoden was shot 4 times – three to the side of the head and once under her chin. Hannah May was shot twice in the head, while Chris Jr. was shot 4 times in the head. Kenneth Rhoden was the only one shot once – through his right eye. The autopsy report also revealed that some of the victims had bruises on their bodies, indicating that they had been beaten as well.

Investigation

Investigators were immediately stumped by the crime. There were numerous questions raised by the crime scenes, but no signs pointing to who may have committed the crime. None of the neighbors reported hearing any gunshots that night, and despite the copious amounts of blood at the scene, there were no prints recovered or items that seemed out of place. The killer or killers' mode of entry into the homes was unknown, since there were no signs of forced entry into any of the houses. The investigators initially theorized that it may have been a murder-suicide, but none of the victims were found with a self-inflicted gunshot wound. The Ohio Criminal Bureau of Investigation set up a taskforce of 100 law enforcement officers to investigate the case, and over 25 sheriff's departments offered support to their Pike County counterparts. The Federal Bureau of Investigation as well as the Drug Enforcement Agency also provided support to the Pike County Sherriff's Office. Just a few hours after the discovery of the first bodies, the largest criminal investigation in Ohio was underway.

On April 24, 2016, the Attorney General of Ohio, Mike DeWine, held a press conference to give an update on the progress of the Rhoden case. He told reporters: "Let me go ahead and, I think it's okay for us to confirm, uh, that we did find marijuana in three locations," and a reporter interjected, "Grow operations?" DeWine confirmed: "Grow operations." There were 200 plants found in the three houses on Union Hill Road, and investigators also found evidence that chickens were getting bred for cockfighting purposes. Investigators stated that they found equipment used for such purposes, as well as some chickens. With all the victims being members of the Rhoden family, the surviving family members were asked to take precautions to ensure their own safety. While it was possible that there was only one shooter, detectives theorized that more than one killer was responsible for the killings, especially since it would have been difficult to subdue Chris Sr., who was not a small man by any means. Additionally, the killings were done methodically, and DeWine maintained that it was a well planned, premeditated, and "sophisticated operation."

The taskforce received hundreds of tips, and the investigators worked around the clock to find answers. However, none of the tips panned out, and the investigators' efforts quickly hit a wall. With no clues left at the scene and the different modus operandi at each scene, investigators considered everyone a suspect. Bobby Jo, James Manley, and Donald Stone were initially considered suspects since they are the ones who discovered the bodies, but the three were quickly cleared after subsequent interviews with the investigators. As the weeks turned into months, investigators ran down leads with no result, and the case quickly turned cold.

On August 20, 2016, DeWine told reporters that the investigators were convinced that the killers were familiar with the Rhoden home, their property, and the surrounding area. This echoed what Dana's father, Leonard Manley, stated on April 26, just four days after the murders. Leonard stated that the killers had to be people familiar to the family, mainly because of Dana's two protective dogs. There was no indication that the dogs had tried to attack anyone during the shootings, and there was no forced entry in any of the homes. Leonard also maintained that Dana had no part in the cannabis business, and that the investigators were just "trying to drag my daughter through the mud, and I don't appreciate that." The Pike County Sheriff, Charles Reader, months into the investigation, told reporters that the investigators were convinced that there was more than one shooter that night.

On May 3, investigators seized the properties of the eight victims, including their mobile homes, cars, tools and any other property they owned for "investigative purposes." Three of the homes were taken to Waverly, where the taskforce command center was located, and the fourth home was transported later. Farm tools and equipment were also seized, and the items were stored together, then later moved to a warehouse that was formerly a chemical processing plant. After weeks of surveillance on the warehouse, WXIX-TV released its report highlighting the lax security in the warehouse. They stated that in the three weeks they were camped outside the warehouse, there were no security guards or armed officers guarding the evidence, and the main gate to the warehouse was open. However, DeWine slammed the report and called the report "ludicrous," maintaining that the evidence was preserved. However, a former prosecutor from Hamilton County responded to the report, stating that any evidence stored in the warehouse would likely get tossed out in court.

On May 12, 2017, the Franklin County Sherriff's Office sent its SWAT team out to a farm 10 miles from the Union Road Hill homes. The farm, located on 260 Peterson Road, just off of Highway 32 in Adams County, was once partly owned by Hannah May's former boyfriend, Edward "Jake" Wagner. The investigators did not search the house, barn or land, but rather focused their efforts on the horse trailers and trailers on the farm. Investigators also searched through trailers parked in a car lot on Highway 41 in Peebles. This search was the first public activity by the investigators since the investigation started, but law enforcement did not reveal how they came to focus on the property owned by Hannah May's ex-boyfriend and his family. DeWine and Sheriff Reader pleaded with the community, asking anyone with information to come forward. They maintained that there were some people in the community who had information about who committed the murders, but for some reason, they were scared. DeWine also stated that obstruction of justice charges would be brought against the friends and family members who helped the killers get away with the crime.

Arrests

On November 13, 2018, over two years since 8 members of the Rhoden family were gunned down in their own homes, Attorney General Mike DeWine called a press conference to announce a major break in the case. He stated: "Good afternoon. We promised that the day would come when arrests would be made in the Pike County massacres. Today is that day. Yesterday, the Pike County grand jury indicted four individuals for aggravated murder with death penalty specifications for allegedly committing these heartless, ruthless, cold blooded murders."

The series of arrests sent shockwaves through the community. In a coordinated operation, 6 members of the Wagner family were arrested in connection with the Rhoden family murders. 47-year-old George "Billy" Wagner III, the patriarch of the family, was arrested in Lexington, Fayette County, Ohio, after law enforcement pulled over the horse trailer he was in. Billy's wife, 48-year-old Angela Wagner, was arrested at the family's home near Piketon, Ohio. Their two sons, 27-year-old

George Wagner IV and 26-year-old Edward "Jake" Wagner, were arrested together during a traffic stop in Ross County. All four were arrested within minutes of each other, as investigators were not willing to have them warn each other and have some skip town. Investigators also arrested Billy's mother, 76-year-old Fredericka Wagner, at the family's horse farm – The Flying W farms. Angela's mother, 65-year-old Rita Jo Newcomb, was arrested at her home. Billy, Angela, George, and Jake were charged with eight counts of aggravated murder, Fredericka was charged with obstruction of justice and perjury (the charges were later dropped), and Rita Newcomb was charged with forgery, perjury, and obstruction of justice. The prosecutors also added charges of conspiracy and engaging in a pattern of criminal behavior to the murder charges.

The Wagners

The Wagner family was well respected in the community, and many of the residents had nothing but great things to say about them. However, after the arrests, stories of shady business practices and abusive behavior were brought to light, as more residents became less afraid to talk. One family member described Billy as an odd person, stating that there was something off with him. He was a cold and hateful person, rough around the edges. No one really knows how his relationship with Angela started, but as the years went by, he became more controlling towards his wife. Both his boys and Angela were scared of him, but George was more like his father compared to Jake. According to the relative, Angela could not leave the relationship because

Billy had already warned her that if she did he would track her down.

Many residents and family members sang Fredericka's praises, describing her as a God-fearing woman who ran a nursing home and did a lot of community service. She helped young disadvantaged children and helped others buy buying them groceries. At one point, she even started a church. However, there was another side to the family. Many stated that the family was very secretive, and there were allegations that there were dishonest practices at the nursing home. After the murders, some suspected that the Wagners had something to do with it, especially after the family sold its land and they moved to Canada. Many residents stated that while Fredericka was considered as a generous and wonderful person, she was also a smart and calculated individual. A family member stated that she knew exactly what she was doing, and her actions were aimed at keeping her family's name clean, and to keep the members from getting arrested.

Investigators believed that the four arrested for murder all pulled the trigger, and the speculation was that Angela was the mastermind of the entire plan. After conducting interviews with members of the Rhoden and Wagner families, investigators believed that the finally had a partial motive for the murders – custody of Hannah May's two children.

Hannah May and Jake

Hannah May Rhoden and Jake Wagner met in the summer of 2010. Hannah May was 13 at the time and

Jake was just shy of 18. The two began dating, and would spend their time between the Wagner and Rhoden homes. In November 2013, Hannah May gave birth to their first child, Sophia. The two had been waiting to start a family, and had plans of getting a big family together. Jake was described as a hands-on father who always made time for his daughter. To provide for his family, he began driving a truck with his older brother George. Jake would always ensure that Sophia and Hannah May were provided for, and he was very protective of the two. The grandmothers – Angela and Dana – were excited to have the new baby to dote on, and Sophia was spoiled by both grandmothers. The family split their time between the two homes, and things seemed to be going well for them.

In early 2015, Jake and Hannah May had their wedding date set, and had gotten their rings tattooed on their fingers. However, in April, Hannah May broke up with him. When interviewed by detectives, Jake claimed that Hannah May had left him because he was working too much, and that he had wanted a stay-at-home wife, but she was not ready for that. No one could ascertain his claims, but his family members all agreed on one thing – Jake did not want to give up on the relationship. Hannah May moved back home, and in May 2015, began dating Frankie's best friend and Hannah Hazel's brother, Charlie Gilley. Charlie was head over heels in love with Hannah May, and would constantly post pictures of the two of them kissing on social media. He was well liked by Hannah May's family, and they thought he was a good fit for her. However, the relationship didn't last long, and the two broke up in July. Hannah May carried on a physical relationship with Jake, but she wouldn't agree to go back to him. She began dating Cory Holdren, and as the year came to a close, she found out she was pregnant, She didn't know who was the father, and the candidates were Jake, Charlie, and Cory.

Jake took Hannah's pregnancy seriously, and promised to take care of them even if the child was not his. He constantly checked up on Hannah May to make sure she was okay, and even bought baby stuff. He was willing to do anything to take care of Hannah May, and hoped that the pregnancy finally meant that they would be together again. Angela seemed to share her son's optimism, and even bought a crib for Hannah's new baby.

However, by the time Hannah gave birth to Kylie on April 17, 2016, the relationship between Hannah May and Jake had become very contentious.

When news of the arrests spread in the community, rumors began spreading that the Wagners killed the Rhoden family members because of the bitter custody battle between Hannah May and Jake. Two to three weeks before the murders, Billy Wagner had tried getting Hannah May to sign documents handing over custody of Sophia to Jake. Hannah May refused. According to various sources, Hannah May wasn't letting the Wagners see Sophia, and this soured her relationship with Jake. He tried to get Hannah May to let his family spend time with Sophia, but she was not complying. Jake became furious, and made comments a couple of times that he was going to kill her. He even said this to Hannah May on a number of occasions. Nobody took the threats seriously, and many chalked it up to his anger. However, after the murders, some wondered whether Jake made good on his threat.

Paternity Tests and Custody

Jake's actions before and after the murders were deemed suspicious by some community members and law enforcement agents. On the night of the murders, Jake had shown up at Dana's home to pick up Sophia for a sleepover. This seemed like a lucky coincidence, but after the arrests, many wondered whether he was just making sure that she wouldn't recognize the killers later on. A week after the murders, Jake filed custody papers seeking custody of both Sophia and Kylie. He maintained that even if Kylie was not his, he should be awarded partial custody since the girls needed each other. Many in law enforcement found it suspicious that the Wagners had compiled the papers so fast, when it usually takes 6 months to a year for families to compile the paperwork needed before filing for custody. In June 2016, Charlie, Jake, and Cory submitted their DNA for a paternity test. It was determined that Charlie Gilley was Kylie's father, and he was granted custody. Jake was also awarded custody of Sophia since he was her biological father. Brentley was put in the custody of his mother, while Ruger Lee was put in the custody of Hannah Hazel's parents.

Aftermath

Rita Newcomb took a plea deal in December 2019, pleading guilty to a lesser charge of obstructing official business in connection with the 2016 murder investigation. As part of the terms of the plea agreement, prosecutors dropped the obstruction of justice, forgery, and perjury charges against her.

Billy, Angela, George, and Jake all pleaded not guilty to the charges against them. They will be tried separately.

STALKED & ABDUCTED : THE TRUE STORY OF BRIANNA MAITLAND

KENDRA HICKS

There are approximately 2,300 United States citizens reported missing every single day. Some of these are runaways, some are misunderstandings, some are hurt or killed, and other just disappear without a trace. The friends and families they left behind are left with just a glimmer of hope that their loved one may one day turn up, which is oftentimes more painful than the closure of knowing your child or friend is in a better place.

Missing persons cases are a popular subject matter for shows like Criminal Minds or CSI: Crime Scene Investigation, but many real life cases don't end in the happily-ever-after seen on primetime. In the real world, these cases are often full of loose and dead ends, muddied by apathetic law enforcement or unclear communication between the victim and those close to them. Of those that go missing, the majority are women, who often present themselves as an easy target for those looking to inflict harm on another.

On March 19th, 2004, Brianna Maitland

disappeared. The 17-year-old girl had just left the Black Lantern Inn in Montgomery, Vermont, where she washed dishes and occasionally served tables, when her car was found abandoned only twenty minutes later. Despite a brief visit from a local police officer, and curious passersby photographing the abandoned Oldsmobile, she was not reported missing for several days. Her parents, Bruce and Kelli Maitland, assumed she was at home, and Brianna's roommate was out of town at the time. Brianna left a trail of clues behind her, but over 12 years later there is still no official story for what happened that night. As the years pass without any major leads, the investigation has petered out and will soon be coming to a close.

Who Was Brianna Maitland?

Brianna Maitland was born and raised in Burlington, Vermont, where she spent the first seventeen years of her life living at her parents' quiet farmhouse. On her seventeenth birthday, she packed up her belongings and moved out on her own, despite her parent's pleas for her to stay another year. Her mother told interviewers that there was no serious issue or conflict that resulted in this decision, but that her daughter was fiercely independent and prematurely ready to venture into the world on her own. Although Brianna's early departure caused many to suspect an unhappy childhood or home life, she and her parents appeared to maintain a good, somewhat close relationship for the months after her move.

Brianna was an attractive girl, easily looking several years older than her young age. She was brunette and slightly petite, at 5 foot 4 inches and about one hundred and ten pounds. All around, she seemed to be a well-liked girl with many friends. Some rumors emerged after her disappearance regarding her moving to a new school district. These rumors blamed the move on Brianna being bullied relentlessly by other girls at her original high school, which motivated Brianna to pick up and move her life to an entirely different area. While these rumors are persistent, Brianna's parents or friends haven't confirmed them at this point.

At first, Brianna moved in with her boyfriend, James, wanting to be closer to a group of her friends that lived over 15 miles away from her parents' community. Moving in with her then-boyfriend seemed to be more a move of convenience than love; it didn't appear that she moved out of her parents' house with the intent of being closer and more codependent with him. She enrolled in a new high school, the same one as these friends, and began to settle into her new living situation. Unfortunately, her new home life was quickly uprooted by arguments with James, who she had accused in letters of having a severe drinking problem. By February 2004, barely a month before she would disappear without a trace, Brianna had dropped out of school and moved to a new house.

Now living with Jillian Stout, a friend she had known since early childhood, Brianna attempted to regain control of her life. The two young girls shared a modest home in Sheldon, Vermont, and seemed to be doing fairly well for themselves. Brianna enrolled herself in a high school equivalency program, hoping to earn her G.E.D. as soon as she would have earned her high school diploma if she had not dropped out. Brianna was reportedly excited about this test, looking forward to a new chapter of her newly independent life. Despite the hardships she had fallen on after moving from her parent's house, Brianna was determined to pull herself up and support herself on her own. Sadly, she would disappear only hours after finishing her exam.

While Brianna was not known as a serious troublemaker, she did drink and party like so many other teenagers do. At one of these parties, only three weeks before the night of her disappearance, Brianna was assaulted by another girl from her high school. At the hands of this girl, named Keallie Lacross, Brianna suffered a broken nose and concussion. Some rumors surrounding this attack suggest that Kaellie or one of her friends felt threatened by the pretty Brianna when she was seen talking to their boyfriend or a boy they were interested in. Although Brianna did press legal charges against Keallie, these were not yet resolved when she disappeared, so they were dropped several weeks later.

This scene cast light on some of the darker sides of Brianna's life. Her boyfriend was likely and alcoholic if not worse, she was bullied and harassed by other girls in her social circle who disliked her, and she likely partook in drugs and alcohol herself. While this isn't unusual for a 17-year-old, many in the community and police force expressed doubt that Brianna was attacked or hurt in some way. Instead, to them, she was just another burnt out, teenage runaway.

The Morning of Her Disappearance

The morning of Brianna's G.E.D. examination, she and her mother, Kellie Maitland, met for breakfast. Kellie reported that there was nothing out of the ordinary at this time, and that she had sent her daughter off to her test with plans to meet up and celebrate with her later.

For her celebration, Brianna chose to go shopping with her mother in the afternoon. Kellie said that shopping was one of her daughter's absolute favorite things to do. She said Brianna could walk into any store, pick the most "avant gard" piece off the rack, and model it like she was on an international runway. Brianna's sense of style was something her mother and many others admired about her. In television and print interviews, Kellie Maitland retells these memories with a clear fondness, holding onto those last final hours she spent with her daughter in 2004.

However, according to her mother, Brianna's shopping trip was cut short. As they were waiting in line to check out at one of her favorite stores, Kellie said that Brianna's attention was caught by something outside the store window. Saying that she would be right back, Brianna left the store.

Kellie is unsure where he daughter actually went; she said that she never saw Brianna enter another storefront on the street. After paying for her items, Kellie exited the store and found Brianna waiting for her at their vehicle. She had no shopping bag from another store with her, and there was no one else nearby that Kellie thought she could have been speaking to.

There are many speculations as to what, or who, drew Brianna Maitland out of the store that morning. No matter what happened, Kellie said that her daughter was visibly upset the entire car-ride home. Wanting to respect her daughter's privacy, Kellie never asked Brianna what had happened earlier that afternoon, but this would be the last time she ever spoke to her beloved daughter. She dropped Brianna off in the driveway of her and Jillian's shared house, and then turned onto the highway to the quiet farmhouse she and Brianna had once both called home.

At home, Briana started getting ready for her

Friday night shift at the Black Lantern Inn, one of the teenager's two minimum wage jobs. At around 3:30 in the afternoon, Brianna left her house in her 1985 Oldsmobile, leaving a note for Jillian assuring her that she would be back home after her shift was over. Jillian found the note when she arrived home, after Brianna had already left for the Inn, but then went away for the weekend without ever hearing from Brianna again.

The Last Known Sighting

The Black Lantern Inn, founded in 1803, closed its doors for good on March 29th, 2015. Remnants of the Inn's events and menus can still be found on Facebook and outdated travel sites. The most recent post on the Black Lantern Inn's Facebook page simply says, "The Black Lantern Inn is closed." The Inn offered an Irish restaurant and brewpub, which featured the Inn's own small batch beer brewed on location. Located in Montgomery, Vermont, a small town nestled between the East Coast's rolling mountains, the Black Lantern Inn drew a combination of loyal locals and transient tourists to its establishment. With a fireplace and public house feel, the restaurant and brewpub offered a cozy retreat for the perfect stag night or romantic getaway on a cold winter night. This is where Brianna Maitland spent her last documented hours.

Friday nights are notoriously busy in the restaurant and service industry, and March 19th, 2004, was no exception. In fact, it was even busier than expected, keeping the staff on their feet for the better part of the night and filling the back of house with dirty dishes and utensils. Backed up on her work, Brianna stayed several hours later than usual in order to finish washing the entirety of the night's dishes.

Sometime during the evening, Kellie and Bruce

Maitland passed the Black Lantern Inn, hoping to stop in and visit Brianna at her new workplace. However, after seeing how busy the restaurant was, and not wanting to embarrass their daughter in front of her coworkers and boss, they continued on their way home. To this day, Kellie regrets not making that stop, if only to see her daughter one last time.

At 11:20 that night, the Inn's staff members were finally done with all of their closing duties. As per restaurant tradition, they all planned to hang out, have a drink, and relax after a hard night's work. Brianna, however, declined, stating that she needed to get to bed in time for her Saturday morning shift at her other job in nearby St. Albans, Vermont.

As far as Brianna's coworkers reported, she left alone from the Black Lantern Inn in her usual ride, her mother's hand-me-down Oldsmobile sedan. Brianna and Jillian's home was about twenty miles outside of Montgomery, but Brianna's vehicle didn't make it further than a mile from the Black Lantern

Inn. And, as far as anyone knows, perhaps neither did Brianna.

Shortly after 11:30 that night, a man driving down Route 118 reported seeing a seemingly empty car parked at a run-down building, known as "the old Dutchburn house." He said the headlights were on, but he didn't notice anyone inside or near the exterior of the vehicle. A little after midnight, another report came in of a stopped car at the Dutchburn house, this time with a turn signal on. Later in the night, at about 4 a.m., an ex-boyfriend of Brianna Maitland noticed the vehicle parked off the road as well. Finally, early the next morning, a group of travelers stopped to examine the oddly abandoned vehicle, even going so far as to take photographs of the unusual scene.

A Delayed Investigation

Daylight revealed that the vehicle had actually been backed into the Dutchburn house, damaging the wooden exterior. By early afternoon on March 20th, a Vermont State Police officer finally arrived at the scene, deeming the car abandoned and having it towed to a local salvage lot. It wouldn't be until March 25th that the oddly abandoned car would be identified as Brianna's Oldsmobile.

Because of a series of unfortunate circumstances, no one noticed Brianna's absence until Tuesday, the 23rd, when Jillian called Kellie Maitland to ask if she had heard from Brianna. Since she was away all weekend, Jillian just assumed that Brianna had made other plans and had simply not returned home yet. It is unknown why her second job, which she was scheduled to work Saturday morning, did not question her absence. It's possible that they just thought she was another teenager pulling a no-call-no-show, too apathetic to formally quit.

As soon as Kellie heard that her daughter had been missing for several days, she began calling everyone she could think of. Despite trying to contact her friends, employers, and other family, Kellie failed to find any information on where Brianna could be. With no leads to go off of, she called the local police to file a missing persons report.

At this point, Brianna's Oldsmobile had been removed from the Dutchburn house almost five days ago. That Thursday, March 25th, Kellie and Bruce drove to the Vermont State Police in St. Albans to submit photos of Brianna with her report. It was then that an officer showed them the photos of the abandoned Oldsmobile on Route 118, and the Maitland's identified the vehicle as Brianna's.

As the news of Brianna's disappearance broke,

questions began to emerge as to why the officer sent to investigate the Oldsmobile had not raised an earlier alarm. The Oldsmobile had been littered with all kinds of Brianna's personal belongs both within and outside of the vehicle, including: two uncashed paychecks, her purse, jewelry, spare change, a water bottle, and, perhaps strangest of all, a lime slice. Vomit, assumed to belong to Brianna, was also found in the car's front seat. News articles, personal bloggers, and other armchair detectives have accused the officer, seemingly unnamed in any public documents, of complete negligence when handling the Brianna Maitland case.

While the Vermont State Police conducted a several month long investigation, they held onto the belief that there was no foul play involved in Brianna's disappearance. The general consensus was that she had run away or been swept up in some kind of substance abuse. Brianna's friends and family continue to believe that she would not abandon her life and belongings like that.

In 2012, a young woman's skull was found on a Vermont highway, showing signs of age and being exposed to the elements for several years. While no conclusive evidence has been able to tie this discovery to Brianna or one of the other missing women in Vermont, it remains a possible sign of her fate.

Recently, on the twelfth anniversary of Brianna's disappearance, law enforcement revealed that they had collected DNA evidence from inside the abandoned Oldsmobile. It is unknown if this DNA solely belonged to Brianna, or if this was new evidence or had been collected during the initial investigation. There have been no public updates related to this potentially new evidence.

Brianna's family maintains a Facebook page dedicated to remembering her and encouraging others to come forward with information about her or other missing persons. Support for Brianna and her family continues to flow in through comments and pictures posted to the page.

Flurry of Theories

Unsolved mysteries, whether they be in the form of everyday murder or the paranormal, are a popular pastime for the average armchair detective. Brianna Maitland's case is no exception. There is no limit to the number of rumors and theories built up around her disappearance, some more believable than others. While there is no official statement on what actually happened to Brianna at this time, by breaking down the most prominent theories we can begin to understand what might have happened that night. While this list is not inclusive of every theory about Brianna's disappearance, it features the most likely or those that are most supported by the case's evidence.

A Drug Deal Gone Bad – One of the more common theories regarding Brianna's disappearance connects the scene of her abandoned car with the shopping incident reported by her mother. It is known that, like many girls her age, Brianna was often seen at parties where alcohol and other substances were being used. Whether Brianna had an issue with any particular drug is unknown, but it's very likely that she partook at least occasionally, and she regular hung out with teenagers who were known drug users and dealers. These facts lead many people, including some police officers, to believe that Brianna was caught up in a bad drug deal or otherwise got on the bad side of some of the area's dealers.

The most common story within this theory is that Brianna owed money to a local cocaine dealer, who she had been avoiding for some time. When out shopping with her mother earlier on the day of her disappearance, Brianna had spotted this dealer or one of their associates following her and her mother around town. This is when Brianna had gone outside, confronting the dealer and possibly promising to meet him later on with the money he was owed.

Later that night, either because the dealer was simply sick of waiting for his money or because Brianna attempted to avoid him once more, things turned violent. What happened after Brianna's car was abandoned is not entirely answered by this particular theory, but it is clear serious harm was done to Brianna Maitland that night or shortly after. Later, a story would emerge that filled out some of this theory's more gruesome details.

Murdered by Ramon Ryans – About three years after Brianna's disappearance, a police report from the Burlington Police Department offered to potentially solve the mystery. This report, given by Debbie Gorton, from Colchester, Vermont, claimed to answer the questions that the Maitland family and law enforcement had been asking for years.

Gorton's statement came about because her sister, Ellen Ducharme, had been charged with the drug-related murder of Ligia Collins. Some speculate that this story was an attempt to throw attention off of Gorton's son, who had recently been arrested for an unrelated crime, but that question remains unanswered.

In Gorton's statement, she claimed that Ducharme had told her about the murder and disposal of Brianna, committed by Ducharme and several of her associates. According to Ducharme, a known drug dealer, named Ramon Ryans, had taken a "couple thousand" dollars from Brianna which she had given him to buy crack cocaine. Brianna, either because she decided she needed the money for something else or because Ryans failed to deliver on the deal, confronted Ryans to ask for her money back. Ducharme told Gorton that Ryans had abducted Brianna on the night of March 19th, when her car was found abandoned.

Ducharme told Burlington police that Brianna was kept alive for up to a week, suffering who knows what kind of emotional and physical abuse at the hands of Ryans and his friends. Brianna was kept in Ryans basement, possibly even past the time of her death. According to Ducharme, Briann's body was dumped at an unknown local pig farm.

It is particularly strange, if this is truly what happened, why Brianna's attackers did not take her money or un-cashed paychecks from her vehicle. If her murder was motivated by money, these would be easy loot. More likely, though, this was a crime of pure rage.

Gorton believed that several people were involved in the murder and disposal of Brianna's body, including her sister, Ramon Ryans, Moses Robar, Darrel Robar, and Timothy Crews. No charges were ever made against these individuals in the case of Brianna's disappearance and the accusations remain uncorroborated by any local law enforcement.

Stalked at Work – It is sadly common for

service industry staff, especially women, to be harassed and followed by their customers. While Brianna's primary role was in the back as a dishwasher, she occasionally served and helped out in the front of house when it was busy.

Another common theory of her disappearance is that she had acquired a stalker in her time at the restaurant, or from somewhere else who had then found her workplace and continued his stalking there. Since Brianna was an attractive, young girl, this theory is not too hard to believe.

Perhaps Brianna was aware of this stalker, though never confided in the police or her loved ones, and this is who she had seen outside the store she was shopping in with her mother. If she had confronted this man and demanded that he leave her alone, this would have made her nervous and on-edge like her mother later described. This rejection by his object of affection may have also sent the stalker into more violent methods.

With this theory, some believe that the man was

hiding in her Oldsmobile's backseat, waiting for Brianna to clock out and head home. Shortly after she had left the Black Lantern Inn, he could have emerged and told her to either pull over or drive somewhere at his command. This also would have explained why the Oldsmobile was backed into the old Dutchburn house, because oftentimes women are instructed to drive into an object in order to stun or hurt an attacker in their vehicle. Unfortunately, if this is what happened, it appears that the stalker was successful in his pursuit of Brianna.

Pregnancy Scare – Fueled by the small town rumor mill, another frequently heard story is one of teenage pregnancy. Playing up Brianna's partying side, this theory suggests that a mistake between two young people turned into a case of cold-blooded murder.

On the day of her disappearance, Brianna already knew that she was pregnant. Maybe she had just found out, or maybe this fact had been weighing on her mind for weeks. Either way, when she left her mother in the store checkout line, Brianna was going out to tell someone about her pregnancy. Whether this was a friend or the potential child's father, Brianna did not want her mother to overhear the conversation and find out that she was pregnant.

Later that night, she had stopped at the old Dutchburn house. The vomit found in her vehicle leads some to believe that she got sick on her way home from work and pulled over in order to clean up or gather herself before continuing home. This is where someone met her, because she asked him or her to or because they had followed her from the Black Lantern Inn, most likely the potential child's father. Either way, this person was extremely unhappy at Brianna's news. Perhaps it was a cheating partner who had gotten Brianna pregnant, or simply a young man who was nowhere near ready for the financial and emotional responsibility of having a child.

The old Dutchburn house is backed by a nearby

forest and river, which can be easily accessed by a short walk. If Brianna was killed at the location of her car, this is likely where her body was left. No trace of Brianna was ever found in this area, but there is always a chance that it was swept away or buried beneath the soil.

A Deadly Party – Following along with Brianna's supposed party girl image, this theory suggested that she had actually made it further than the old Dutchburn house that night. However, as we'll see, there are some discrepancies throughout this theory that make it highly unlikely.

After leaving for work that Friday, rather than going home to rest for her morning shift like she had told her coworkers, Brianna had driven out to a nearby party. Here she was either involuntarily drugged or willing took drugs herself. As the night progressed and intoxication levels increased, Brianna began to overdose. Unable or unwilling to get her the appropriate help in time, Brianna died that night at the party. Afraid of being caught, and potentially charged with the murder of Brianna, those at the party secretly disposed of the body. Later that night, her car was planted in order to look like it had been abandoned or that something had happened to her on the side of the road. If a couple drunk teenagers were driving Brianna's vehicle to the old Dutchburn house, this could also explain the vomit found in the passenger seat of her car.

The most obvious hole in this theory is the sightings of Brianna's parked car at the Dutchburn house less than an hour after she had clocked out of work at the Black Lantern Inn. This timeframe would leave her no time to get to a party, let alone overdose and have her vehicle planted by other partygoers. However, witness sightings are notoriously inaccurate, leading some to believe that the initial sighting of Brianna's Oldsmobile either didn't happen, was a different car pulled over on the side of the road entirely, or happened at a later hour and the witness was either mistaken or lied to the authorities.

For those who see Brianna as a wild, high school drop out who ended up hanging out with the wrong crowd, this story might be very easy to believe. Even law enforcement were quick to say that Brianna's disappearance was more likely an accident than premeditated foul play. Brianna's close friends and family don't believe this tale, though, and hold onto the belief that Brianna was an innocent victim the night of her disappearance.

A Victim of Human Trafficking – Human trafficking is an often overlooked issue in the United States, with many believing that it only occurs in foreign, third world countries in Asia or Europe. While most known cases of human trafficking occur at airports, large metropolitan areas, and other locations with a high volume of travellers and business, some do occur in small towns or seemingly innocuous places like coffee shops or malls.

Women are the most common victims of human trafficking, usually being sold into the nonconsensual sex trade. While the men, or "Johns," who visit these women are rarely aware that the sex worker they are visiting is actually being held against their will, these women's captors can be violent, abusive, and frequently end up killings their prisoners. Some human traffickers will also force their victims to develop a drug addiction, often to heroin and other hard street drugs, so that they are more easily manipulated and apathetic to their situation.

    Those who believe that Brianna, likely targeted because of her petite, non-threatening figure and good looks, was sold into sex trafficking believe that she was smuggled over the nearby Canadian border. This would explain why her personal belongings, such as I.D. and jewelry, were left behind; the abductors would not want any identifiable information with her in case they were caught. However, it's strange that none of her money was taken if this was the case.

Final Blow From Kaellie Lacross – While Kaellie Lacross's, the girl who had attacked Brianna at a party just three weeks before her disappearance, charges were eventually dropped, she remained the primary suspect in many people's eyes. After all, it is quite possible that a grudge strong enough to assault someone over is a grudge strong enough to murder someone, purposely or not, over.

Whatever it is that triggered Kaellie's attack at the party, it's not impossible to believe that she wasn't satisfied with the outcome. If Kaellie was intending to teach Brianna a lesson, whether it was to not speak poorly or her or to stay away from particular boy, she might have felt the need to scare Brianna even further. Knowing that Brianna worked at the Black Lantern Inn, Kaellie could have followed her and forced her to pull over on the side of Route 118.

Here, Kaellie, likely the help of her peers, could have threatened Brianna and physically attacked her again. Whether this attack was meant to kill Brianna doesn't matter, only that it eventually did. Realizing that they had made a huge mistake, and would now be charged with not just assault but with murder as well, the group quickly disposed of her body. They could have placed the body in another vehicle, taking it to a different location, or carried her back into the secluded woods behind the old Dutchburn house.

If the motivation behind this attack was only to scare Brianna, then they would have had no interest in taking her money or other belongings. This theory is supported by having a clear motive, though there is no official report on what the conflict between Brianna and Kaellie was, and if it was serious enough that Kaellie would gone through the trouble of practically hunting Brianna down to resolve it.

The Mystery Remains

Despite this exhaustive list of theories, there is

really no way of knowing what happened to Brianna until someone comes forward with new information. As the Maitland family and Montgomery community approach the thirteenth anniversary of Brianna's disappearance, there are plans to scale back the search for her and what happened.

Up until now, the Maitland family and Vermont State Police have funded a $20,000 reward fund for any information that leads to the discovery of Brianna Maitland, but after all these years with no solid leads, the plan is to donate the fund to a missing persons advocacy group sometime in 2017. Although the Maitland's have not given up hope, they are ready to take a step forward in grieving their daughter, no matter what has happened to her.

The Brianna Maitland Facebook page remains active, wishing followers happy holidays and posting alerts for other missing persons cases. Serving as a memory of Brianna, whether she remains alive or not, the page aims to draw out information on her case and the thousands of other missing persons cases that go unsolved every year. Brianna's case has also been featured on several true crime podcasts, television shows, and blogs, hoping to unearth the answers to questions that everyone has been asking since that cold night of March 19th, 2004.

THE DISAPPEARANCE OF KELSIE SCHELLING

ANA BENSON

Every time a woman goes missing or is found murdered, the police usually takes a closer look at their spouses or boyfriends. It is a standard procedure, especially if there were indications that they were in a troubled relationship. The disappearance of Kelsie Schelling is one of the biggest mysteries in Colorado. This young pregnant woman was last seen in February of 2013 and the case is still open to this day.

However, Kelsie's family was quite disappointed at the lack of interest by the police to investigate her then-boyfriend Donthe Lucas, who was clearly involved in this crime. After all, Donthe did invite Kelsie to his hometown on that fateful night and he was the last person who saw her alive. When they realized that the police are stalling with the investigation, the family made a promise that Kelsie's case will not be forgotten until they discover what really happened. They kept the public informed through their Facebook page and eventually managed to reach the Colorado Bureau of Investigation.

Early life

Kelsie Jean Schelling was born on 18th February 1991 in Holyoke, Colorado. She grew up in a tightknit family and later became even closer to her mother after the divorce of her parents. Kelsie was only eleven years old when they split up but she would often talk to her father as well. However, they didn't see each other that often because he moved to a different part of town. After graduating from high school, Kelsie attended Northeastern Junior College located in Sterling, Colorado. She was fascinated with psychology and planned to major in it once she gets accepted to the university.

Kelsie was friendly and outspoken, so it comes as no surprise that she had many friends and was a life of every party. During her time at Northeastern Junior College, Kelsie met Donthe Lucas. He was a star player on the basketball team and the two of them fell in love instantly. Donthe Lucas had a very difficult childhood and he grew up in Pueblo, Colorado which is an infamous place known for higher crime rates than anywhere else in the state. He loved basketball and it was clear that he would be an outstanding athlete even in high school. Basketball players do have enormous salaries so Donthe Lucas did see it as an opportunity to help his family out further down the line.

He was hoping that a scout would attend one of his games and recruit him for one of bigger colleges or universities that had a good basketball team. But his big break never happened. Instead, he ended up in Northeastern Junior College which was alright, but Donthe wasn't quite happy with that outcome. His dissatisfaction was evident even in the relationship with Kelsie. Their romance had constant ups and downs, and the two of them would break up, and get back together which drove Kelsie mad. They did finally call it quits after several semesters, and didn't see each other for quite some time.

After finishing the two years at the junior college, Kelsie pursued her education even further, and she moved to California to attend Vanguard University in Costa Mesa. She was finally able to study psychology full time. Donthe continued to play basketball for Emporia State University in Kansas. Kelsie's family was happy she managed to end her relationship with the troubled basketball player, and they hoped that she would make a new life far away from Colorado. Kelsie was independent and she enjoyed living and studying in California. When she wasn't attending classes, Kelsie worked at a tanning salon with her best friend. However, she did drop out of the college because the school work was a bit too much for her at the time and her only option was to go back home. She moved to Denver in 2012 and started working in a store. Meanwhile, Donthe Lucas was back in his hometown Pueblo.

The two of them started talking once again during the autumn of 2012. It was obvious that they still had feelings for each other, so no one was surprised when Donthe and Kelsie decided to spend the Christmas holidays together. The couple seemed happy to everyone around them, but Kelsie did tell her friends that their relationship was still very toxic. Donthe was still treating her badly, calling her names, and starting unnecessary fights. Soon enough everything will change. A few weeks after the holidays, Kelsie found out that she was pregnant. Shocked at first, Kelsie was lost and decided not to tell anyone for a couple of weeks. But keeping a secret was hard. So she called her mother and told her the news. Kelsie's mother Laura would later say that even though her daughter felt a bit stressed, she was still excited about the pregnancy. Yes, she was young but Kelsie was determined to make it work.

Donthe Lucas didn't take the news so well. Having in mind how dissatisfied he felt about his failed basketball career, it is not wrong to assume that the news about a baby simply solidified the fact that his dreams will never come true. Kelsie noticed the change in his mood and openly told him that he doesn't have to be a part of their baby's life. But it is also worth mentioning that Kelsie confided in her best friend that Donthe was ecstatic to become a father at one point. However, his mind was constantly changing. Kelsie went to see her doctor on 4th of February 2013 and he confirmed that she was eight weeks pregnant. The baby was healthy and doing well. The doctor provided her with an ultrasound of the unborn baby, and she was full of joy. Kelsie immediately sent out the pictures to her mother, her friends, and Donthe. Unfortunately, the excitement will not last forever.

The night of the disappearance

Donthe and Kelsey exchanged several emails on February 3rd, 2013. He invited her to visit him in Pueblo.

She turned him down saying that she needs to go for a checkup the next day to make sure everything is alright with the baby. After seeing her doctor on the morning of February 4th, 2013, Kelsie went straight to the store. She worked the second shift and was expected to come home sometime after 10:00 PM that night. However, she was in contact with Donthe for the entire day, texting back and forth about the pregnancy. Donthe told her that she should drive out to Pueblo after work because he had a surprise for her. Not knowing what it is, Kelsie asked for more information because Pueblo is two hours away from Denver, and she would probably be tired after work. He insisted that she would be happy with his surprise and that he cannot tell her anything over the phone.

It is safe to assume that Kelsie thought that Donthe was ready to change and start a family with her. Their relationship wasn't a standard one but it seemed like Kelsie was willing to move past all the negative things and focus on the future. So after her shift ended, Kelsie got in her Chevy Cruze LTZ and drove to Pueblo in the middle of the night. Donthe was supposed to meet her in a parking lot in front of a local Walmart. The surveillance cameras did confirm that Kelsie got there on time, but Donthe was nowhere to be seen. She waited in a parked car for almost an hour before sending another text message to Donthe, saying that she has been in the parking lot for too long and that she would come pick him up at whatever location he is at the moment. She got a reply sometime around 12:15 AM.

Donthe told her that he will be waiting for her in the street next to his grandmother's home. Kelsie is seen exiting the parking lot a couple of minutes after she got the message. She clearly did arrive at the second rendezvous spot, but once again Donthe wasn't there. Kelsie sent him another message asking where is he and Donthe replied that he will be there in a minute. This is the last known communication between these two until sometime before 04:00 AM. After going through the phone records, police did discover that Donthe called Kelsie at 03:54 AM but she didn't pick up. The significance of this mysterious phone call will be revealed later. After reviewing the cell tower pings for both phones, the investigators did discover that they were in close proximity to each other.

The search for Kelsie

Kelsie's mother Laura got really worried the next

day because she wasn't able to reach her daughter over the phone. She tried calling numerous times but it went straight to the voicemail. The last message she got from her daughter was the ultrasound image of her unborn child, and Laura wasn't sure if something happened to Kelsie after work, or she was ignoring her calls. Laura contacted Kelsie's friends who told her that she went to Pueblo to meet with Donthe. With no word from her daughter, she called Donthe who picked up his phone and told Laura that he had seen Kelsie last night, but that she drove back home in the morning.

    Laura was starting to panic, but she did tell Donthe that she would involve the police if she doesn't hear from her daughter soon. Laura and Kelsie were very close and they did tell each other everything, but she suspected that her daughter kept this information from her because she didn't want Laura to know that she was meeting with Donthe. After all, Laura was aware of the nature of their relationship, and his reluctance to accept the baby. Plus,

Laura would probably advise Kelsie not to go to Pueblo in the middle of the night.

Laura contacted the local law enforcement and told them that her daughter was missing. Without any solid leads or evidence, they started asking around for Kelsie. Their first step was to take a closer look at Donthe because he claimed that he was the last person to saw Kelsie. She did travel from Denver just to see him. After checking Kelsie's credit card records, they did notice that the card was used hours after Kelsie's last known contact with Donthe. They reviewed the surveillance of the ATM and noticed that Donthe had the card and picked up $400 from Kelsie's account. They weren't sure if Donthe had Kelsie's agreement to use the card, but that was a felony in the state of Colorado, so he was led to the police station for questioning. He had a lot of things to clear up, starting with the timeline of Kelsie's visit to Pueblo.

Donthe's interview

After being picked up by the police, Donthe told his

own version of the story. They did see each other that night and talked until early morning hours. Donthe and Kelsie got into a fight and she felt too agitated to drive back home to Denver. She was also very tired from working the second shift. Instead, Kelsie decided to sleep in her car which was parked near his grandmother's house. According to Donthe, his phone rang sometime around 07:00 AM and it was Kelsie. She wasn't feeling well and asked Donthe to drive her to a hospital. He put on his clothes, got to her car, and drove her to the Parkview Hospital.

Kelsie wasn't sure if something happened to the baby during their argument last night and she insisted to see a doctor before she heads out to Denver. Donthe sat inside her car in the parking lot for two hours when she finally emerged from the hospital. Kelsie told him that she had lost the baby. She then asked Donthe to drive her to Walmart to get something to eat and buy some snacks for the road. The two of them started fighting while they were in Walmart and Kelsie refused to drive him home. Donthe simply walked away and got to his grandmother's house on foot. He didn't see Kelsie later in the day and he assumed she went home. He didn't mention stopping at the ATM to pick up the money during his initial interview.

The investigators did notice a couple of possible leads that could collaborate Donthe's story, namely the Parkview Hospital. Each medical facility keeps detailed records of the patients they treat. After speaking to the staff and going through the data, they have confirmed that Kelsie didn't check in during the morning of February 5th. There were also numerous surveillance cameras all over the building and none of them picked up Kelsie entering or leaving the hospital. It was obvious that this part of Donthe's story was not true.

Of course, the police investigators decided to check out Walmart as well because the parking lot and stores do have surveillance cameras, and they might have picked up something that would be of use. While they couldn't find Kelsie or Donthe entering the Walmart, they did notice Kelsie's car on the parking lot. However, the timeline didn't match up with Donthe's story because Kelsie's car appeared at noon, and not in the morning. Plus, Donthe was the only passenger in the car. Another surveillance camera which was positioned on the back side of Walmart did record Donthe getting into his mother's car – another detail he failed to mention in the initial talk with the investigators.

Without any proof that Donthe's version of the events is true, they called him up for a second interview. The investigators did have a plan this time - they wanted to find out more about the ATM, and how it fits into his timeline. He told the detectives that he took $400 in order to pay his bills and that Kelsie lent him the money since he was at the ATM while Kelsie was at the hospital. When the detectives told Donthe that there is no record of Kelsie ever being in that hospital, his reply was: "I don't even know what to say right now."

They also presented him with Walmart surveillance video that proves Donthe was the only person in the car. He was surprised with the evidence put in front of him, and before the detectives managed to get him to open up, he decided to lawyer up. He was only charged with the identity theft due to the fact that he used Kelsie's credit card, but the case was dropped. The judge had determined that Donthe did use Kelsie's credit card in the past and it was a normal behavior. However, nobody managed to figure out why Donthe had her card in the first place. After all, if Kelsie decided to ran away and start a new life, she would need the money, as well as her vehicle.

Speaking of Kelsie's car, the investigators took a closer look at the surveillance video from Walmart parking lot because they wanted to follow the vehicle. Exactly one day after Donthe left Kelsie's car there, another man approached the car and got inside by using the key. He didn't break in or steal the car. The man was dressed in black, wearing a hoodie, so identifying him was almost impossible. His body type was different than Donthe's, and the mystery man was significantly shorter. Keep in mind that Donthe was a tall basketball player, so his height would be noticeable, even in a low-quality video.

Seeing the direction in which the car went, the police collected the surveillance videos from stores and businesses which were in close proximity. They put the puzzle pieces together and found a route but they couldn't follow it all the way. One day later, the car was dropped at the parking lot of Saint Mary Corwin Hospital. The man locked the car and walked away. The investigators located the vehicle on 14th of February, 2013 and figured out the timeline. But nobody knows where the car was during 6th of February. There weren't any signs of a struggle that would indicate that Kelsie was killed in her car. Almost all of her personal items were missing, including her wallet and a backpack.

While it is unclear if the vehicle was tested for the traces of DNA, an unnamed police officer who worked for Pueblo Police Department will later say that they did find bodily fluids in the trunk of Kelsie's car, as well as two palm prints. However, no one knows what happened with this evidence and was it ever tested. It is simply another thing which the police investigators decided to ignore in this case. Unfortunately, the whole investigation will be under scrutiny soon after.

Theories

Figuring out a solid theory without too many evidence or information can be challenging. Laura, Kelsie's mother, claims that her daughter was probably murdered and that it was premeditated. The first red flag for her was Donthe's initial invitation to meet him before the doctor's appointment. When Kelsie refused, he knew that he had to act fast. Donthe lured Kelsie to Pueblo by saying that he has something to show her, but he never gave an explanation to the law enforcement about what the surprise really was.

It is clear that Kelsie was alive and well up until the point she met Donthe in the street next to his grandmother's house. This is where the trail goes cold. The activity on her phone stops until 04:00 AM. If we analyze the location of the phones, another theory is that Donthe led Kelsie to a remote location and harmed her. It was possible that Kelsie dropped her phone in the middle of a struggle. Donthe couldn't find the phone in the dark, so he had to call her number. He was very likely getting rid of the evidence.

There is a possibility that the two of them did indeed get into a fight, and that an unfortunate accident happened. However, it is more likely that Donthe planned to get rid of Kelsie, and had planned every single step he would take that night. He really insisted to see her as soon as possible. While it is not fair to put the blame on the rest of Lucas family, the fact that his mother picked him up immediately after he left Kelsie's vehicle at the Walmart's parking lot indicates that she knew what was going on. Pueblo Police Department did stop investigating Donthe, and they claimed they didn't have enough physical evidence to prove that a crime really occurred. But they did receive a couple of noteworthy tips which were ignored and never pursued.

The missed opportunities

The entire investigation of the disappearance of Kelsie Schelling was troubling from the very beginning. While the detectives did not have physical evidence of a crime, it was clear that Donthe was the last person who saw Kelsie alive. In every standard investigation, he would have been the prime suspect, and the investigators would do their best to find more proof that he was somehow connected to the crime. The cell tower pings did show that both of their phones were in a remote area next to Pueblo in the early morning hours.

But there are even bigger missed opportunities that could have provided the investigators with the proof they needed. For instance, Donthe was living in his grandmother's house at the time of Kelsie's disappearance. However, the entire family moved out soon after. The landlord started redecorating the house because he wanted to rent it again. He did hear about the missing girl from Denver but had no idea about the details of the case, or the fact that the Lucas family was involved in any way.

He decided to put the new carpets in and when he lifted the old one, the landlord noticed a strange stain on the bottom. He contacted the police enforcement because he was worried that something bad has happened in the house. However, the police ignored his request to check out the stained carpet, and no one had ever arrived at Lucas' previous residence to pick it up. The landlord ended up throwing the carpet away because he simply couldn't keep it forever in the house and wanted to move on with the renovation.

Another missed opportunity involved a couple of fishermen who were out on a lake on a night fishing expedition. It is important to mention that the lake was located near the Saint Mary Corwin Hospital. As you might recall, that was the spot where the police officers discovered Kelsie's vehicle on the 14th of February 2013.

They were out on a bank when a hook got stuck to something poking out of the sand. The fishermen went to investigate and were sure that they saw a part of a human ribcage, as well as a skull.

They were terrified by that discovery and left the area right away. Both of them were reluctant to notify the police because they did have some troubles with the law in the past. But that didn't stop them from telling this story to their friends who urged them to contact the local law enforcement. A couple of months passed before they finally talked to the police, but the lake wasn't searched afterward.

The current searches

Family and friends continued to search for Kelsie

even after it was clear that the police enforcement forgot about her case. They created a Facebook group that was constantly updated with new information. Pueblo Police Department did go through many changes after Kelsie went missing. The lead investigator was replaced with a new one who was willing to cooperate with the Schelling family. The Schellings did offer a large reward for any new leads that might help them locate their missing daughter. The reward was $100,000 at one point.

This eventually led to false claims and misleading messages such as the one which claimed that Kelsie was still alive, but was placed into a sex traffic ring after a hired hitman decided not to kill her. Laura Schelling contacted the police and told them about the message. Since the investigators decided to follow every lead possible, they dug deeper and even involved the FBI. Their experts did manage to trace the message back to Russia through the IP address so it was clear that this tip was useless.

The biggest break in the case happened in the

spring of 2017 when Colorado Bureau of Investigation finally got the authorization from the local law enforcement to join the search. CBI did determine that the prime suspect should be Donthe Lucas, and they got the warrant to search the area around his previous place of residence. A large number of police officers was seen around that house during April of 2017, and they dug up the parts of the backyard using heavy machinery.

The search has been successful and the officers left the scene carrying bags of evidence. However, they stated that they didn't find any traces of Kelsie's remains. Kelsie's family released the following statement after the search: "The past 2 days have been grueling and emotional, ending with the outcome we did not hope for. Kelsie is still missing. There is no way for me to convey to you all the pain that I feel right now. Sincere, heartfelt thanks goes out to the members of Pueblo PD, CBI and Parks & Rec who worked so hard on this search for Kelsie. This was a physically demanding excavation for them and we witnessed how hard they worked. Despite all the issues we have had in the past, the new leadership over Kelsie's case from PPD and active involvement from CBI is giving us hope that an effective investigation is finally taking place."

The case is still active and the police didn't arrest Donthe. But the positive changes are happening and Kelsie's family is certain that they will find the answers they are looking for now that the investigation is finally moving forward.

THE DISAP-PEARANCE OF BRITTANEE DREXEL

FAITH TORINO

Brittanee Drexel disappeared from Myrtle Beach, SC while on spring break on April 25, 2009. She was 17 at the time and traveled without receiving parental consent. She told her mother that she was staying at a friend's house near their home in Rochester, New York. Brittanee's mother, Dawn, then learned where she really was when her boyfriend, John, called her after he suspected something had happened to Brittanee. Her parents immediately grew angry, scared, and devastated when they received word that their daughter was missing.

Brittanee was born on October 7th, 1991 and lived in Rochester, New York. She moved frequently during her youth as her father was in the military. She was a junior at Gates-Chili High school and the year was a rough one with her parents separating. She would live with her mother but still see her father frequently.

She was blind in her right eye and had several surgeries to correct her hyperplastic primary vitreous. To keep her eye from wandering, she would get contacts that made both eyes look the same.

Britt was described by friends and family as a smiling, fun-loving girl. Her demeanor had changed by her junior year in high school as she was depressed that her parents were separating. She would sleep in late and begin to skip school. She would overdose two times on her mother's pain medication and both times were fueled by the fact that she had just broken up with her on-again, off-again boyfriend, John Grieco.

"I felt it was all my fault," Brittany's father said. "When I was here none of this went on. She didn't ingest as many pills as they thought but still watching her get her stomach pumped was a warning. I need help."

"I remember the look on her face," Dawn said. "She was all red. She was crying, tears coming down her face. 'Why would you do this? Nothing in life is that bad.'"

Brittanee would be forced to see a counselor after the suicide attempt. Still, things seemed as if they were a mess on the home front. Her parents were separating and her mother was losing her home. But she would resume her studies at school and excel on the soccer field.

"She was fast," her father said. "Her coach would say he'd never seen a girl that fast."

By the time Spring Break rolled around in, she was ready to go on an adventure with some of the older kids she knew. It was a long-standing tradition for Rochester students to go to Myrtle Beach for vacation. Britt wanted to enjoy the night life and lay out in the beach, so when one of her older friends asked if she wanted to come along she didn't hesitate.

She asked her mother first and the idea was immediately shot dawn. Dawn Drexel did not know any of the friends that would be taking Brittanee.

"She asked me and I said 'no'," Dawn recalled. "Then she went to talk to her father. She would play us both. She would say Mom said 'no' but Dad said 'yes'."

Brittanee was determined to go. She pleaded with her mother once again and was turned down. Angry, the two got into a fight and Britt would call her boyfriend to come pick her up.

Brittanee decided to fool her mother. She told her mother that she wanted to stay at a friend's house nearby for a couple of days. Dawn reluctantly agreed but Brittanee headed off to South Carolina instead.

Dawn believed that someone had offered her something, like a "modeling job or some other kind of ruse" to get her to go down there. She had aspirations of being a model as well as getting into cosmetology. With her striking good looks, she would be a shoo-in for success in the modeling profession.

"Her biological father was Turkish," Dawn said. "She had a very European look."

Defying her mother, Brittanee would visit her boyfriend at his workplace and tried to entice him to come along. The young man declined, stating that he had to work.

Brittanee then left with her older friends Jennifer Oberer, Phillip Oberer and Allana Lippa to Myrtle Beach. Jennifer was twenty-one years old. Her brother Phillip would be charged with rape in an unrelated case (charges would be dropped) in 2010. It is believed that these were considered the 'cool kids' and that Britt wanted to hang out and be liked by them.

Britt texted her boyfriend numerous times

throughout the trip, telling him about the ambience. She expressed her love for the hot weather, palm trees and the happy vibe of young people finally away from parental supervision. But according to friends and family, Brittanee didn't know the older kids that well.

She also called her mother and lied, telling her that she waswatching movies at a friend's house.

CHANGE OF HEART

Britt hit the clubs with her friends and her mood quickly changed. Her friends began using a lot of drugs and she didn't want any part of that scene. She went off by herself, checking out the local shops and walking down the beach.

She then met up with a friend from Rochester, a man named Peter Brozowitz. He was also in town and staying at the Blue Water Resort with his own group of friends; Matthew Abrams, Philip Watson, Keith Cummings, and Anthony Schimizzi. The 20-year old Brozowitz was a "club promoter" who got Brittanee into Club Kryptonite. The next morning, she would meet Peter again at the beach.

The next day, Brittanee called her younger sister and told her that she's at the beach. Her sister believed she's at the local beach which is only twenty-minutes away. Britt then has a friend to impersonate the parent of the friend get on the phone to talk to her mother. The friend assured Dawn that everything was okay.

Britt then got back on the phone with her mother.

"I'll see you tomorrow," Britt said. "I love you and I'll see you tomorrow."

It would be the last time Dawn would ever speak to her daughter.

THE MYSTERY OF WHAT HAPPENED THAT NIGHT

Brittanee decided she would meet up with her friend Peter that night. She borrowed a pair of shorts from a friend and headed out. She texted her boyfriend John, telling him that she's having a miserable time and that she doesn't like the people she went down with. Apparently, they were 'mean-girling' her after she didn't do drugs with them.

She then received a text from her friend who stated that she wants her shorts back. Irritated, Brittanee walked back to the hotel to return the item.

At least that is what her friends say happened as Britt would disappear into the night.

John then became worried when Britt did not text him back. He texted her a few more times, waited, received no answer then he threatened to tell her mother that she's in South Carolina if she doesn't respond back.

Convinced that something is wrong, John calls Dawn at home. He explained that Brittanee is in Myrtle Beach.

Dawn went livid but her anger soon turned to concern when Britt didn't respond to her own texts or calls.

Everyone in Brittanee's family was notified. Something was wrong. Terribly wrong.

The next morning Dawn, her parents and John all made the trek to Myrtle Beach to try and look for

Brittanee.

THE SEARCH BEGINS

Police in Myrtle Beach were notified and questioned the friends that Britt had been staying with. Their answers were all the same, they had not seen Brittanee since last night. Police also turned to Dawn, questioning her about Brittanee's state of mind.

Would she run away? Had she done this before?

There was no indication that Brittanee had motivation to do such a thing. Nor did they have any reason to believe she was doing a lot of drinking or drugs.

With no other leads, detectives turned their eyes on the last person to have seen Brittanee, Peter Brozovitz.

Peter would make an appearance on the Dr.Phil show and proclaim his innocence. He stated that they were in his hotel room watching the Yankees-Red Sox game when Brittanee was engaged in a texting argument with Jen Oberer who wanted her shorts back.

He said she didn't have a problem with walking a mile back to her own hotel.

Brittanee's parents were on the show and berated Peter for not "being a gentleman" and driving her back to the hotel. They also found it suspicious that Peter and the rest of Brittanee's friends did not do more after she was missing.

"I had spoken with Peter that morning," Dawn said. "He was giving me three different scenarios...It's fishy."

Peter responded angrily, stating that he was 'being

thrown under the bus.' The innuendos were clear, that even if he had nothing to do with Brittanee's disappearance, she went missing because he didn't look out for her.

What is suspicious is that Peter had abruptly left Myrtle Beach with his friends around 2 a.m, five hours after Brittanee had vanished. They left clothing behind in their hotel room and looked to have been in a rush.

Upon his return to Rochester, Peter hired a defense attorney.

Peter had told investigators that she left his room shortly upon arrival to return the pair of shorts to her friend. The detectives got a hold of the surveillance camera from the hotel and verified Peter's story. At precisely 8:48 that evening she was seen leaving Peter's hotel to return back to her own hotel. She should have shown up on a traffic camera about fifteen minutes away but she never made it that far. She was abducted somewhere along that street.

Police continued to question Peter. The young man stated that one of his friends was told by his mother to return home immediately. This story was corroborated and law enforcement did not pursue the matter any further.

Instead, they now focused on Britt's cell phone.

Britt's last text message to her boyfriend was around 8:58. Ten minutes after she had left the hotel she texted "I'm packing and going to sleep probably."

This would be the last outbound message she sent as then John began texting her repeatedly with no answer back.

But the calls she received from John and her friends were pinged by her cell phone. Every time a friend called, her cell phone communicated with the nearest tower.

In looking at her cell phone records, she was moving southbound. The last ping was received at the Poleyard boat landing.

Fifty miles away from Myrtle Beach and two counties over.

Whoever abducted Brittanee knew exactly where they were going. The place was isolated, a rural country islet that only fishermen or locals would know about.

This was not the kind of place a seventeen-year-old girl would go to on Spring Break.

The investigators launched their search in the area that was about four miles in radius. Unfortunately, the terrain was treacherous. Alligators, wild hogs, snakes and biting insects the size of golf balls populated the area looking for their next meal.

Four-wheelers were brought in to keep the alligators away from the sniffing cadaver dogs. Investigators came to the site armed to shoot any wild hogs that came near.

"If her body is here," one investigator told Dawn in an ominous tone. "She would be eaten within six hours."

The search was frantic in the beginning but investigators seemed to lose hope after a few days passed. Britt's family returned home to Rochester with sunken hearts.

Brittanee's little brother chastized her friend upon their returning, stating "I thought you were bringing Brittanee back!"

Eight months later, police still had no promising leads. They would get an anonymous tip to check out an area a few miles north of the original search area near the Scantee River.

Once again, they came up with nothing. But a couple out fishing found a pair of sunglasses that looked as if they would belong to a teenage girl.

Neither her parents nor her boyfriend recognized the sunglasses as belonging to Brittanee. A DNA test was performed on the glasses and nothing was found.

Her mother continued to believe that she's alive.

"I think she was taken and held against her well," Dawn said. "I think she has become the victim of human trafficking."

Investigators and reporters shot down the notion, however. Typically, human trafficking occurs where the victim has a language barrier and Myrtle Beach was not exactly a hot bed for that type of crime. The police did not rule it out but it is low on their list of possibilities.

From 1997 to 2010, South Carolina has reported 12 cases of documented sex tracking. All were women, according to Doors to Freedom, an organization that helps victims of sex trafficking.

A few months later, police would receive some cell phone footage of Brittanee shot by a young man she had met. There were a group of teens antagonizing her and she wanted the young man's help to hang out with her so they would stop. He shot some footage of her sitting by herself, texting her boyfriend. He has since been cleared of any suspicion as he did have an alibi.

Pressed for suspects, law enforcement looked at every possible lead.

Three years later, authorities identified fifty-one year old Raymond Moody as a person of interest. They obtained a search warrant for a Georgetown motel room where Moody rented out at the time of Brittanee's disappearance. They noted that Moody had received a traffic ticket in Surfside beach just one day after Brittanee went missing.

Moody was a a registered sex offender, having raped a nine-year old girl in 1983. He was released in June of 2004. But Moody did not cooperate with investigators and remained tight-lipped under interrogation.

He is also a suspect in the case of Crystal Soles who disappeared in January of 2005.

"We've heard his name before," Dawn Drexel said. "It's a possibility the cases are connected. We don't know what happened to Crystal or Brittanee."

Moody lived in an area where Brittanee's cell phone last pinged. He was referred to as "Mr.Clean" because of his resemblance to the bald character in the Mr. Clean commercials. He has not been mentioned in any police reports since 2012, however.

The FBI would get involved and offer their belief

that Brittanee was abducted and taken to a "stash house" where she was raped and then murdered. Her body was then wrapped in plastic and she was thrown into an alligator pit where her body would presumably be eaten.

    This narrative was offered by FBI Agent Gerrick Munoz who obtained the informaton from an inmate named Taquan Brown. Brown is serving a 25-year sentence for a different case but stated he was present during Britt's last moments.

    He said he had seen Britt when he visited a "stash house" which was a moniker used by drug dealers to describe a place where they stashed weapons, money or drugs.

    Brown stated that Taylor picked Britt up in Myrtle Beach and took her to McClellanville. Once there he "showed her off, introduced her to some other friend that were there...they ended up tricking her out with some of their friends, offering her to them and getting a human trafficking situation."

    The stash house was in the McClellanville area, the last location where Britt's cell phone was pinged.

    Brown told the officials that he saw Da'Shaun Taylor, who was 16 years old at the time, and several other men "sexually abusing Brittanee Drexel."

    Brown then claimed he went to the backyard to give Da'Shaun's father money.

    During this time, Britt tried to escape. She was caught by one of the men who "pistol whipped" her across the head. She was then taken back inside the house.

Brown stated that he heard two gunshots and then saw the woman being wrapped up and removed from the home.

The FBI agent revealed that "several witnesses" have told him that she was dumped in a pond that was filled with alligators.

Taylor has since been convicted of robbery in 2011 and could face a life sentence. He stated that he knows nothing of Britt's case and with the lack of evidence he has not faced any charges in her disappearance.

Chad Drexel, however, thinks Taylor may have been involved.

He recalled a time when he was out handing out Brittanee's missing person fliers and handed it to Taylor who was in his car.

"I gave him the flier," Chad said. "He had a car full of brothers, friends. He handed the flier to one guy in the back seat. They all laughed and then drove away and threw the flier out the window."

"I got mad. I said 'There's something about this guy...'"

After the information was released to the public, Taylor's mother, Reverend Joanne Taylor, immediately defended her son.

She stated that he had already served his time for the robbery (a McDonald's restaurant) and that he was a "great kid" that was only 16 years old at the time of Brittanee's disappearance. During her son's hearing, Taylor's mother took the stand and said the following:

"And I want to say that at the time of this alleged abduction, he was 16 years old. I was never a mother thatwould let my kids run loosely, and definitely not with the father, you know, out to do things. I kept great hold on him. I am a pastor of a church. They were in church, they had a strict bedtime, I knew every place that they went. MyrtleBeach would not be a place that he would go at the age of 16. So I just, you know, I ask for your fairness, I ask for, you know, the correct justice in this case. And know that he is not a flight risk. I mean, I teached them good values, I instill in them what few things that have happened, they have exemplified overall what I've taught them. He is not, you know, a flight risk or anything.

Chad Drexel read the testimony and immediately took to his own Facebook page.

> *I would like to set the record STRAIGHT with a STRONG REPLY to Joan Taylor's comments to the Post Courier in South Carolina this past Friday.*
>
> *Based on evidence the FBI and the Myrtle Beach Police department has gathered, along with FACTS and SPECIFIC INFORMATION gathered from a team of Private Investigators that I HIRED to work with local law enforcement actively during the case (which will SOON COME TO LIGHT) – we have no*

doubt Timothy Da'Shaun Taylor played a significant role in the abduction and murder of my daughter.

Of course the mother of Timothy Da'Shaun Taylor is going to defend her son – as a father I can understand a need to defend your children. What I DON'T understand is defending your children when you must KNOW the truth. Her assumptions and words stated have been verified INCORRECT and couldn't be farther from the TRUTH. We know Timothy Da'Shaun Taylor was witnessed by others (Witnesses NOT IN JAIL) with my daughter – we are just praying that they do the RIGHT thing and stop forward with what they know. Additionally he has been seen and followed to the EXACT area where my daughter's DNA was found. Joan Taylor claimed that the FBI and government are falsely accusing her son because of witnesses IN JAIL?! Well, we have other specific evidence, that I can NOT disclose at this time for the safety of my daughters case, which corroborates these testimonies!! Timothy Da'Shaun Taylor is KNOWN to be involved in dog fighting, bringing drugs to parties, and raping women (mostly Caucasian young women) he either picks up UNWILLINGLY or friends of friends that end up being drugged and taken there. This IS ONLY THE BEGINNING!! There is a TON more "EVIDENCE and HORRIBLE INFO" we would like the PUBLIC in that area be aware of for their safety, but we are unable to disclose at this time.

WITHOUT A DOUBT ....Timothy Da'Shaun Taylor is a suspect in my daughter's Disappearance and Murder! My family and I will be following the FBI's requests to keep specific details in our daughter's case under wrap until THIS HORRIBLE PIECE OF TRASH goes to Prison for Life. After the guilty verdict, we will be happy to dispel these fairy tales that are being spun by Timothy's family. It is disgraceful the way this FAMILY and their FRIENDS are supporting and claiming innocence of a "PROVEN" FELON without even looking at the evidence presented and the FACTS surrounding the case.

Also adding this PIECE OF TRASH photo so everyone can see WHO HE IS!

On March 25th, 2017, FBI agents called Dawn Drexel to inform her they may have located Brittanee's remains. They are now searching an area 45 miles north of their previous search spot.
After two days, however, they gave up the search.
The case is ongoing.

MISTY COPSEY

Misty Copsey was fourteen years old when she disappeared on September 17th, 1992 after a trip to the Puyallup Fair.

Her case remains a showcase of administrative screw-ups and dropped balls. She was initially thought of as a runaway before foul play was finally suspected a month after the fact. Subsequently, there have been at least five people suspected of committing her abduction.

But the Puyallup police did not get within sniffing

distance of Misty or charging anyone with her disappearance. Three different police chiefs and numerous detectives all took a swing at the case and whiffed. No one in law enforcement has been able to answer the question on everyone's lips.

What happened to Misty Copsey?

A GOOD GIRL

Misty was born in 1978 to Diana and Paul "Buck" Copsey. Her father was a firefighter but the couple split up shortly after she was born and Misty lived with her mother.

Misty got good grades in school, excelling particularly in Math. During her last quarter at Spanaway Lake Junior High School, she got A's and B's. Athletic, she played softball, volleyball, and basketball before breaking both forearms during an athletic practice.

Misty was not the ringleader of a bad crowd. She was diffident but funny, entertaining her friends while skipping around and singing the theme song to Sesame Street.

She did not have much in regards to material wants. Her mother eked out a living as an in-home care nurse and they lived in a mobile home park until she was fourteen. Seeking a better place to live, Diana and Misty moved into a duplex where she now had her own room. But Misty longed for her friend who lived in and around the old trailer park. She would make it back there when she could to just hang out.

Tall, blonde and with green eyes, Misty was cute enough to draw the attention of boys. She remained chaste, however, and was not dating like so many of her other friends.

Her innocent, girl-next-door looks would draw the attention of Rheuban Schmidt. Rheuban looked like a casting call actor for a meth head. He sported a reverse mullet, a hairstyle that was cut close to the sides with curls on top. He had beady, green eyes that screamed low IQ. One of Misty's friends described him as a "scuzzy looking dude" but he nonetheless befriends Misty, much to the chagrin of her mother.

Diana grew suspicious of the relationship as Rheuban was four years older and a high school dropout. On one occasion, she listened in on the other end of a phone conversation Misty was having with Rheuban.

"I get horny just looking at you, Misty," Rheuban said, whispering like an old pervert.

Diana became enraged and ordered her daughter off

the phone.

"Don't ever talk to that idiot again...."

ENTER CORY BOBER

Cory Bober was a thorn in the side of police every since the Green River killings became a national news story. He would insist that the police are "incompetent fools" while organizing his own searches for her remains. Diana would later accuse him of killing her daughter but he would respond by telling Diana that she was being "ungrateful." He was, after all, the only man on the case.

Bober was a recluse without a vehicle or a drive's license. An inveterate marijuana user, he had a record for both possession and dealing. He was also obsessed with cases of murdered or slain women in his home state of Washington. He had a stack of binders with autopsy reports, pictures, and other arcane details.

Bober came under the radar of the police in Puyallup when he became obsessed with the Green River Killer case. He had a brief acquaintance with Randall Dean Achziger, remembering a conversation where the man told him that the killer inserted rocks into the remains of his victim. Bober became suspicious as that would turn out to be a piece of information only known to police. He then went on a one-man crusade to prove the guilt of Achziger. Bober would interview his ex-girlfriends, friends, co-workers and present all of this in an affidavit to the courts.

Achziger found it ridiculous and annoying.

So did the police.

The Green River Killer would turn out to be a painter named Gary Leon Ridgway.

Bober didn't give up, however. He knew Achziger was the guy.

Bober had his own theories about who was performing the killings. Some were wild and outlandish conspiracy theories. Others were spot on. He would notice that there were victims that "had disappeared on the very same date that others were discovered. Some victims seemed to almost 'commemorate' the deaths or discoveries of others; one would die on a particular date and another would disappear a year to the day later on the very same date."

The police dismissed his theories as the rantings of a crack head. But Bober would be willing to show the proof of his connect the dots calculations. He pointed to the cases of Kim Delange, a 15-year-old killed in 1988 and Anna Chebetnoy, a 14-year-old killed in 1990. Both of their bodies would be found along Highway 410, east of Enumclaw.

Bober discovered that the remains of both girls were found in the same section of 410. The girls were found two years and one month apart. He felt that the killer was following a pattern.

He called the police department and left a voice mail. He predicted that a teen girl from Puyallup would disappear and her remains would be found on Highway 410 in the same vicinity where the other girl's bodies were found. Bober gave him the name of the man whom he felt was the serial killer.

Randall Achziger.

But the police were now used to his calls and viewed him as a crank. A nutcake with a strange vendetta.

His prediction would be half-right, however.

There would be no body found on Highway 410.

But a teenage girl would disappear.

Her name was Misty Copsey.

A NIGHT AT THE FAIR

On September 17th, 1992, Diana told her daughter Misty and her best friend Trina Bevard to behave themselves. Misty had convinced her mother to let them stay out that night...free of any meddlesome adults. But Trina's guardian would not allow her to go without an adult driving them home.

Diana worked as a caregiver for a 97-year-old Alzheimer patient who could not be left alone. She would not be able to drive the girls home. But Misty checked the bus schedules and convinced her mother that they would be okay. There was a bus that left the fair at 8:40 p.m.

Misty then convinced her mother to lie to Trina's guardian, Marlene Shoemaker.

"No worries," Diana said to Marlene. "I'll bring them home."

She wanted to be the cool parent, different from the stuffy adults who forgot what it was like to be fourteen. If it meant telling a white lie so her little girl could have some happiness, so be it.

What was the worst that could happen?

Diana dropped the girls off and gave them one last warning.

"Get home safe."

It would be the last time she would ever see her daughter again.

THE PHONE CALL

A few hours later, Diana would then receive a phone call from Misty as she tended to her elderly patient. Misty told her that she had missed the bus but could get a ride from Rheuban Schmidt.

Diana, knowing what kind of unsavory character Schmidt was, adamantly refused. She told Misty to find someone else to give her a ride back. Misty had an electronic diary which she used to store phone numbers. She told her mother she would find someone trustworthy to call for a ride.

"You call me back when you find someone," Diana said.

"I will. I promise."

Diana would wait all night for the phone call.

In the ensuing hours, Misty would not call back.

Worried, Diane called home in the hope that Misty had gotten a ride without calling her.

No answer.

Diana didn't panic. She figured that Misty went home with that scumbag Schmidt and didn't want to get yelled out for disobeying her.

She's going to get yelled at either/or. All Diana wanted was for her daughter to be safe.

Her shift finally ended and Diana drove back home in a rush.

Upon entering her house, she called out for Misty.

Silence.

She went into Misty's room and saw that it had been untouched from the previous night.

Diana would call the police in a panic. She told them that her daughter had not come home from the fair. The dispatcher would tell her that the police could not do anything about it for thirty days as it "sounded like a runaway case."

Diana knew otherwise.

Trying to calm herself, she figured that Misty was with Trina, that the two of them would be okay.

She called Trina's home.

No answer.

She then began scorching the earth with phone calls.

She would call Rheuban but he told her that she called but he didn't have the gas to go get her. She then called numerous friends of Misty and her mother.

No one had seen Misty.

She called Trina's home again, got no answer, then drove out to her house. She then went to the police department and filed a formal report with the Pierce County's Sheriff's Department who handled runaways as opposed to the Puyallup Police.

MISTY'S MISSING

Misty's friend Trina called Diana after she came back from school. She told the frantic mother that she didn't know where Misty was.

"The last time I saw her, she was heading for the bus," she said.

Diana would call Rheuban again. She would get his roommate this time, James Tinsley.

Diana needed answers. She interrogated the young fifteen-year-old like a grizzled police detective. She asked if Rheuban had been home all night. James then told her that Rheuban and his uncle went to pick up Misty but that he wasn't home just yet.

Later, Diana would call back and Rheuban would tell her that his roommate got the story wrong. He went to a party instead and didn't pick up Misty. He didn't know where she was.

Diana pleaded for the police to do something. They dragged their heels and began talking to some of Misty's friends. "Just call if she calls," they informed them. "No one gets in trouble."

Diana printed fliers with Misty's picture. She plastered them in and around the fairgrounds while calling the media.

The one woman search team would yield no leads. Rheuban would stop by and ask if the police had found anything yet. Diana would then wait at the bus stop near the fairgrounds to inquire with different drivers on the route. She found one driver who said that he saw Misty. She had asked when the next bus to Spanaway was arriving. The driver said it wasn't and that he was done for the night. He gave her instructions on which bus to take but she walked away before he could complete his sentence.

AN ERROR OF JUDGEMENT

Among the many mistakes that the Puyallup police made in the investigation of Misty's disappearance was to make the assumption that she was a runaway. Why they didn't entertain the prospect that she could have been kidnapped and murdered gave the abductor precious time to cover his tracks.

The police came to this erroneous conclusion after they interviewed Misty's mother, Diana. They thought she was a liar and an alcoholic. They then interviewed a pair of Misty's classmates who really didn't know her that well or accompany her to the fair.

A series of cover-ups then ensued, as the police told the media Misty had been found (where they got that information remains a mystery) and made no further investigation.

Until Diana and the media started to make a fuss. The department had to save face and eventually one of the detectives believed that this was not a runaway case.

Misty's disappearance could not be ignored any longer.

Police would talk to the various fair workers and security guards. No one had recalled seeing Misty.

The police then turned to her family, interviewing and doing background checks on both Misty's father, Buck, and Diana.

Their impressions of the duo would support their initial theory that Misty runaway. Diana was an alcoholic with multiple DUIs and seven years prior she had been convicted of welfare fraud. Buck confirmed that his daughter and Diana would have their issues.

Carver then discovered that Diana had filed a runaway report on Misty a month prior to her disappearing.

Diana would later state that the report was wrong. She thought Misty had disappeared then found her in the bedroom. She was too ashamed to tell the police it had been a false alarm.

With the police questioning and media coverage, Misty Copsey was now the talk of her Spanaway Lake Junior High school.

Rumors would abound at the school, one of which came from Misty Matthews who said that Misty had called her from Olympia. Another student stated that she saw Misty at a Color Me Badd concert at the fair.

The rumors were enough to prompt Carver to remove Misty from the FBI's National Crime Information Center as a missing person. He would once again treat her as a runaway.

BOBER'S THEORY

Cory Bober's knew he was right. He knew that police would find a body of a young woman off Highway 410.

He waited but nothing happened.

Until his mother showed him the flier of Misty's disappearance.

Right again!

Heart racing, he called the number on the flier. Bober would get into contact with Diana and hurriedly told her all about his research.

He talked about the Green River Killer, where and how he killed his victims. He would tell Diana that her disappearance was connected to the same guy responsible for the murdered Puyallup Girls, Kim Delange and Anne Chebetnoy.

Cory would apologize to Diana because he knew that Misty was dead. He predicted her body would be found somewhere along Highway 410.

The two would form an uneasy alliance. Bober became Misty's personal avenger. He would start a phone/letter/media campaign to prove the police wrong and himself right.

Misty was no runaway.

She was a victim of Randall Achziger.

In October, however, Bober would be arrested for selling marijuana. He was then accosted by Sgt.Herm Carver who tired of the young man meddling in police affairs.

"He walked in the room I was being held in – looking tired and pissed off. He said, 'I got out of bed tonight, and came down here to meet you – just to see what kind of a hypocrite you REALLY ARE!'

I said (being cocky), 'It's not MY FAULT – HERM – that you don't believe Misty Copsey's MISSING!!'

He yelled (angry), 'DON'T YOU EVER CALL ME BY MY FIRST NAME – IT'S SGT. CARVER TO YOU!!!'"

Bober's journals, November 1992

THIRTY DAYS MISSING

Sgt. Herm Carver and Deputy Brian Coburn would each individually warn Diana of the troublemaker that Bober was. Still, the worried mother would welcome his assistance as she needed all the help she could get. After numerous phone calls, the two would finally meet after a month of Misty being missing. Diana had nowhere else to turn but to the shaggy-haired twenty-six-year-old who lived with his parents.

The police were going through the motions on their end. Carver reactivated Misty's name on state and national lists but only because he was legally required to do so. At this point, he still believed Misty to be a runaway and doubted Diana's veracity.

Meanwhile, Diana would find Cory Bober's constant badgering to be annoying. It got so bad she filed a restraining order against him.

"My daughter has been missing for six weeks from the Puyallup Fair," Diana wrote in the restraining order. "Cory Bober has called me on a daily basis, telling me my daughter is dead. I was advised by Deputy Brian Coburn to file this complaint if I felt threatened."

The order would only last two weeks. Diana would then call the courts and rescind her request. She would later call Bober and apologize. Her daughter had been missing for over 56 days. Bober was annoying as hell but he was the only one doing research. The only one who cared.

Bober organized a volunteer search for Misty in the

Green River area. He somehow coerced someone on the police forensic team to tell him the general vicinity of where one of the Puyallup girl's body was found. Bober surmised that Misty's body would be found in the same general area.

Seventy-two days after Misty had gone missing, there was now a volunteer team searching for her.

Nothing came out of the search.

But Diana would later spot Rheuban at a grocery store and confront him. The young man ran and got into a truck with an older man. She saw the look of fear and apprehension on both men as they sped off.

Diana would then lapse into a depression. She tried to commit suicide with booze and prescription drugs.

The next day she would wake up in a hospital. She would spend the next day there, drying out until being discharged back into the nightmare that had become her life.

A PLEA TO THE PUBLIC

Four months after Misty's disappearance, Diana would appear on a local TV station for a special on the Green River Killer. Jim Doyon, the homicide detective who worked the case, spoke of the killings but deferred on stating if Delange and Chebetnoy(the slain Puyallup girls) were connected.

Doyon took an interest in Misty's case. He would journey to Highway 410 and search near milepost 30 where the bodies of Delange and Chebetnoy had been discovered.

Like Bober and the volunteer search team, he too came up empty.

Bober was undaunted and organized another search. He realized that they had been searching in the wrong spot. They were searching on the south side of the highway when the should have been searching on the north.

Twelve people would show up for the search. Diana would arrive with her older sister, Debra. Bober would arrive with Al Hensley, the father of one of the slain Puyallup girls along with his 14-year old Boy Scout nephew, Jaremy Brown.

It would be the Boy Scout that would make the find

Poking into a ditch with his stick, he saw the crumpled blue jeans. Socks fell out of the jeans.

Baggy and stone-washed, they were cuffed at the bottom. The same jeans that Misty had borrowed from her mother on the night of the fair. The jeans were too big for her and Diana remembered them cuffing them on the bottom.

Bober became excited. He knew that the killer had planted the jeans there as a taunt.

He was right. The police were wrong.

But Diana, according to her sister, "broke into a million pieces."

THE KILLING FIELD

Seven dead women had been found in the nine-mile stretch between Enumclaw and Greenwater in the eight years prior to Misty's disappearance.

The two slain Puyallup girls were found in the same area in 1988 and 1991, only one hundred feet apart. They were left off a footpath that had been hidden by thick brush.

Both of the teenage girls had been presumed abducted from the Puyallup shopping center. Detective Jim Doyon believed privately that the cases were connected. He arrived at the site where Misty's jeans were found and interviewed witnesses, particularly

Diana and Bober.

The jeans were taken to the lab and the forensic analysis indicated that the jeans had been in the ditch for some time.

Police suspected that someone (Bober? Diana?) had planted the jeans there.

What was undeniable that the jeans were found only a ten minute walk away from where the bodies of the two slain Puyallup girls were found.

SUSPICIONS ARISE

People began to talk. There were reporters who believed the jeans were planted there. Some were talking as if Diana and Bober were lovers and had plotted this for some insurance money.

Dede Miles, a fifteen-year-old friend of Misty, would come to Sgt. Carver with a tip. She said there was a boy that kept coming over to Misty's parties. He would always leave before her mother came home.

His name was Rheuban Schmidt.

Finally, the unkempt looking young man would come under the radar of the police.

Diana, meanwhile, began to suspect Cory Bober.

How did he know where to look? Why was this stranger so interested in the case to begin with? How did he know so much?

The police had warned her to stay away from him. Now she felt compelled to tell the police of her suspicions.

"Diana comes to station. Now feels Cory Bober may be involved in Misty's disappearance. I asked Diana to submit a written statement to that effect and why she feels he may be involved – she agreed to do so."

Carver's notes

AN INTERVIEW WITH TRINA

Detective Jim Doyon would interview the fifteen-year-old Trina Bevard, the last person to see Misty alive.

Six months had passed. Doyon had brought along the jeans with him, the sight of which made Trina cry.

"It seems to me like something that Misty was wearing that night," Trina said. "It looks very close to what Misty was wearing. The socks, they match what she was wearing. The jeans are big, so – her jeans were baggy that night, that she was wearing. They're – they were light blue like they are in the photo. It just seems, you know, it was the clothes that she was wearing."

Doyon would go on to ask what she was wearing (a pullover) and if she had any jewelry. He then asked if she had any cigarettes or birth control pills.

"No," Trina said. "She was straight. She was a virgin. She didn't smoke, she didn't drink, she didn't do drugs. She was clean, so she had no reason to do anything. She wasn't sexually active."

Trina then revealed that the girls made five calls to Rheuban. They could not get a hold of him. They finally got him on the line and he still refused to pick them up even when the girls offered him money. Misty told him about a key under the front doormat of her home. He could go inside, get money for gas and come pick them up.

Trina stated that she didn't trust Rheuban but only because he didn't keep his word and come pick them up. She then called a 23-year old friend named Mike Rhyner for a ride but they got disconnected. The girls were then stranded. They walked downtown to get to the bus stop before spotting a phone booth by a convenience store. Misty then called her mother, telling her that if Rheuban didn't come pick her up she would take the bus. The two argued as Diana didn't want

Misty around Rheuban.

Trina had to get home by 10 p.m. She had about an hour and a half to get home which wasn't that far. Misty could not walk the ten miles to Spanaway.

Trina then decided to walk. She gave Misty her extra money for the bus.

"At that time I made my decision of walking home and she said she would take the bus," Trina recalled. "The last words that I said to her were 'Be careful,' and she turned around and told me the same and we walked off in different directions"

Trina also dismissed the notion of Misty being a runaway.

" Her mom just bought her a stereo and she was so excited and she went shopping and she got new clothes,"Trina recalled. She was telling me all about it. She was really excited about it.

BOBER GOES TO JAIL

Meanwhile, Bober would be sentenced to fourteen months in prison for the marijuana possession. He felt that the sentencing was too punitive and threatened law enforcement that they would never find Misty without him. His fellow inmates thought he was crazy and began calling him "snitch" and "The Green River

Killer".

Jail would not slow down Bober's efforts, however. He continued to research and write Misty's mother.

"Dear Diana,

...When we found Misty's clothes, part of me died and I watched a part of you die too (much more than a "part") and I was at a total loss for words. I never wanted to be the one to show you your most horrible fears were true and that your daughter is truly dead at the hands of a sick murderer. I will never rest until the killer (Randy Achziger) is brought to justice and dead, if it takes my life to do it."

AMERICA'S MOST WANTED

Misty's case would eventually be broadcast nationally as it was featured on the America's Most Wanted television show.

Over twenty-eight tips came into Sgt. Carver from people who watched the broadcast.

When the tips went nowhere, Diana's suspicions returned to her original suspect, Rheuban Schmidt. She wanted Carver to speak to the young man but the Sergeant would take a circuitous route to get to Schmidt.

Carver would speak to Frank Rodriguez, the owner

of Adam's Ribs, a restaurant where Rheuban worked. He convinced the owner to try and find out how much Rheuban knew about Misty.

"3-4-93 @ 1500: Frank states Rheuban said the following during a lengthy conversation about Misty Copsey:

- Yeah, I know about it.

- I know exactly where she is buried.

- They found the clothes but she is buried 6 miles from there.

- They're off by 6 or 6 1/2 miles."

— Excerpt from Carver's notes

Carver would then wait for Rheuban outside the restaurant before his shift started. Schmidt arrived, saw the cops and immediately ran off. The detectives would eventually catch up with him.

Rheuban would concede that he had received calls from Misty the night of her disappearance. But his story corroborated with Trina's, he told the girls he had no gas and could not pick them up.

Carver then asked if he knew where Misty was buried but Rheuban was adamant that he "said those things to get Frank off my back."

Rheuban then revealed that he suffered from "black outs". He stated that he did not recall anything until the daylight hours of September 18th, 1992.

The detectives pounced, asking if it was possible that he blacked out, picked up Misty and harmed her.

Rheuban claimed he didn't know.

All he knew was that he drove out to his grandmother's farmhouse and couldn't recall why.

Detectives would then give Rheuban a polygraph test.

They would later state that the suspect "zoned out" during the test, nearly falling asleep. The tests were inconclusive but detectives felt as if he were trying to beat the test.

A LITTLE LIE

Rheuban fell off the detective's radar when Carver talked to Dede Miles again. Dede would tell the detective that Trina had not walked home from the fairground like she told him.

Dede said that Trina had a boyfriend come pick her up and didn't want anyone to know.

Trina's boyfriend's name was Michael J. Rhyner. He had nothing on his record aside from traffic stops but he had friends that were connected with Chebetnoy and Delange.

He also had a complaint when he was sixteen years old. He was accused of an abduction rape wherein he used a knife and a cigarette lighter to terrorize an eleven-year-old.

Charges were never filed for an undisclosed reason.

Carver brought Trina in for more questioning. He wanted the truth. The truth about who picked her up that night. The truth about Misty.

But the truth was that Trina told the Sgt. Carver and Detective Tom Matison that she lied because she feared "getting into trouble with her guardian about it."

Trina admitted that she called Rhyner, got disconnected and left a message. She told Misty that they could both ride with Rhyner but Misty said no.

"Trina would not be specific why Misty did not trust Rhyner, but the indication was that Rhyner might have 'come on' to Misty at one time and she did not like it. Trina states that she and Rhyner are friends, but not involved."

— Matison's notes

Trina said that she started to walk and then Rhyner picked her up and dropped her off. The detectives asked if perhaps Rhyner had picked up Misty but she said no.

FRANK RODRIGUEZ' FOLLOW UP

Diana would state that Frank Rodriguez, Rheuban's employer, would call her to say that Rheuban had "bragged about doing something" to Misty with his uncle. Frank didn't fully believe him, however, as Rheuban was "weird" and always bragging about stuff he didn't do.

Diana then approached Carver about Rheuban and the sergeant went ballistic.

"We have our man!" he said.

The man he sought was Michael Rhyner, Trina Bevard's boyfriend.

"We share our knowledge of Mike Rhyner and how he is involved with Misty and Trina – and the fact Trina lied to Doyon. We state that there is an excellent possibility that Rhyner may be linked to Chebetnoy and DeLange. Exchange of information is extremely beneficial."

— Carver's notes

"Sgt. Carver believes that Rhyner dropped Bevard off, returned to the area of the fairgrounds, located Misty Copsey, convinced her to get into his vehicle and drove off with her."

— Doyon's notes

Police set up a sting on Rhyner. The car mechanic was selling his 1981 blue Ford Escort for $200 bucks.

The buyer was an undercover cop.

He watched as Rhyner hurriedly took out trash from the car before the sale. The police then did a forensic examination of the car.

Meanwhile, Rheuban's green Nova was being crushed at a wrecking yard. The Puyallup police didn't care as the tweaker was no longer on their radar. Also, Randy Achziger, Bober's suspect, had been charged and convicted for the rape of a seven-year-old.

INTERROGATING RHYNER

Ideally, Detectives Matison and Sgt. Carver wanted the forensics back from Rhyner's Escort before they spoke to him. But the wait became interminable and they brought him in for questioning without some evidence to back up their suspicions.

Rhyner's story would match that of Trina's. He picked Trina up and went back home. He said that he and Trina were only "good friends" and he had met Misty only four times. Matison then asked Rhyner if he felt Misty was alive and what should happen to the person who harmed her.

Rhyner knew what the detective was getting at. On his own volition, Rhyner told the detectives about his juvenile complaint from years ago. He stated he had been cleared and knew that was why they were looking at him now.

"First thing I thought, you know, well, that's in my file," Rhyner said. "Now you guys are going to think I did it since it's in my file. About Misty, that's the one thing that worried me."

Rhyner then passed a polygraph test.

Grasping at straws, the police then turned their sights back on Rheuban. If only they had impounded his car when they had the chance...

TOO LITTLE TOO LATE

"Rheuban Schmidt's initial interview with Sgt. Carver and I created more questions than answers. He was very vague about what he did that September 17th and finally said that he had a 'blackout' and 'woke up' at his grandmother's property near Enumclaw.

…Schmidt had told Frank Rodriguez that Misty's body was six miles from where the jeans were found. He now claims that he said this just to get Rodriguez "off his back," and was not a true statement.

He was driving a Green Chev Nova at the time but he no longer has the vehicle. It was repossessed.

Schmidt also mentioned that his Grandmother's property is located in King County by Buckley and is over a hundred acres. The property has cows on it. Few people enter onto the property."

— Matison's notes

Tinsley, fifteen years old at the time of Misty's disappearance, told police the Rheuban was his roommate for only a few months. He described Rheuban as a short-tempered guy who had a thirteen-year-old girlfriend. The girlfriend, Tinsley said, got jealous when Rheuban got a call from Misty.

Tinsley stated that Rheuban had left the apartment in a huff then came back between eleven and one at night.

So Rheuban did not "black out" as he told detectives.
N

"What do you think might have happened to her?" Matison asked.

"Um, I couldn't, I couldn't say because I have no idea," Tinsley said.

"Well, can you speculate?"

"With Rheuban, this is just that I, this, this is what I say with Rheuban because I, I figure that um that he, he tried to, he tried to um, get with her or something and she said, she said no and he got all pissed and did something, I don't know, that's just a second guess."

"You think Rheuban would be capable of ah, kidnapping and killing somebody?"

"I think he could," Tinsley said.

Detectives would meet with Rheuban again, relaying the information that Tinsley recalled him coming back to the apartment that night.

But Rheuban remained adamant in stating that he didn't remember what he did. The detectives then drove him out to his grandmother's farm which had over 100-acres...100 secluded acres.

Detective Matison would note that Rheuban's

grandmother's house six miles north of Buckley. Rheuban told Frank that Misty would be buried six miles away from where her jeans were found which would place it in the close vicinity of his grandmother's farm. They would go to inquire with his grandmother but she was not home.

They did not follow-up with the grandmother .

Even so, Rheuban's story no longer held up. He told Misty that he didn't have any gas. He lived sixteen miles away from the fair.

But then he stated that he had driven to his grandmother's farm in Buckley then returned home.

A sixty-mile round trip.

Detectives would give him another polygraph test which he passed.

"It appears that Rheuban Schmidt was not involved in the disappearance of Misty Copsey. He, however, has no alibi as to his movements during the evening of her disappearance, as well as no memory; he claimed that he had a blackout. He acknowledges that he left the residence of James Tinsley, but does not remember what he did.

Investigation to continue."

— Matison's notes

ONE YEAR ANNIVERSARY

The local media ran a few more stories on Misty's disappearance as the Puyallup Fair started. The forensic test on Rhyner's test finally came through. There was no match

with Misty anywhere.

Now once again grasping at straws, Carver would turn to Diana and her associates. He would interview Diana's parole officer and one of her ex-boyfriends.

Misty's father, Buck, was asked to take a polygraph test. He gave consent and passed.

"I explained to her that missing person investigations, at some point in time, must eliminate the parents of any wrongdoing. Diana agreed to the examination."

— Carver's notes

Diana would pass her polygraph test but Jim Corey, Doyon's colleague, said that Diana's polygraph would prove to be inconclusive and that perhaps she had something to do with planting the jeans at the location on Hwy 410.

Carver had always had his doubts about Diana and felt that she planted the jeans.

But the leads would eventually dry up. After nine years, Misty Copsey's disappearance would turn cold.

No one was ever charged with her disappearance.

THE AFTERMATH

Diana would hand out fliers at the Puyallup Fairgrounds every year.

She was doing more than law enforcement and even the media.

Every now and then, a local reporter would run a story about Misty. A few cranks would call in and say that they knew something but it would lead to nowhere. Then that would be it. Everything would run dry.

Detective Jim Doyon felt that she was deceased.

BOBER TO THE RESCUE

Bober was then caught for marijuana possession again but this time, he pressed for an advantage. He would gain the Washington State Patrol crime lab report on Misty's jeans, compiled after their 1993 discovery.

He argued that the lab report was part of his

defense....he gambled and won.

Obtaining the prized document, the amateur sleuth went to work. The report stated there was no blood, no semen. But there were hairs, fibers, and three red paint chips. There were also holes in the left leg in the jeans, above the knee.

Bober knew that somehow, someway, Randy Achziger was involved. That he killed Misty.

The forensic details raced through Bober's head...red paint chips...red paint chips...

He knew that Bober had a red Porsche. He knew that the paint chips would match.

But the police had another suspect they didn't tell anyone about.

Robert Leslie Hickey.

Hickey's hunting ground was the Puyallup area where he specialized in abduction rapes.

He also drove a red Camaro.

Puyallup police had him on their list as a possible suspect but he was never questioned nor did they obtain forensic samples from his car.

Thirteen years later, however, they would collect

samples from Achziger's old car. The car had been sold and the new owner was open to having forensics performed on it.

The particles would be sent to a crime lab which already had a backlog of over a year.

With nothing else left to do, the police turned once again to Rheuban Schmidt.

"I think it's worth taking another shot at Schmidt, and we're planning on it. He's been clean since 1993 ...

— Excerpt from notes by Lt. Dave McDonald, March 19, 2006

Only Schmidt had not been clean. He had been convicted of second-degree theft in 2000. In early 1996, he was accused of rape by one of Misty's best friends. He had held a pillow over her face to silence her but two weeks after filing the report, the girl back away from her accusation and did not file charges.

"[She] told me that she would be undergoing counseling related to the rape, but that she did not want to undergo any additional stress that may be caused by further investigation or possible prosecution in this matter.

Case cleared exceptional/refused by victim."

— Pierce County sheriff's report, Feb. 6, 1996

Later in 2006, Puyallup police gathered more reports on Rheuban. One was a domestic violence protection order requested by his wife, the mother of his three children.

"Rheuban has previously told her that if she ever had him served with a court order he'd 1) burn her house down with her and her kids in it, and 2) send 'some guys' to kick in her door and take money from her.

(She) said Rheuban told her that they'd get money from her if they had to beat her, rape her and then rob her.

(She) said Rheuban told her that if it came to that she 'wouldn't be breathing' when they were done with her."

— Pierce County Sheriff's report, Nov. 9, 2006

MISSING PAINT CHIPS

Adding more incompetence to the investigation, the red paint chips found on Misty's jeans would turn up "missing." All that remained inside the bag where the chips were marked was a piece of plastic.

The lab technicians now had no way to match the red chips on Misty's jeans to Achziger's red Porsche.

Bober would claim that the red chips did match and the police were now trying to save face. Diana, however, no longer wants anything to do with him.

Bober would state that the police would tell Diana that they had, in fact, tested the red paint found on Misty's clothes against Achziger's Porsche. Bober discovered that the red paint was missing beforehand yet the police would lie to Diana about the test.

The lies and incompetence that began investigation have seemingly ended it as well. The Puyallup police relied far too heavily on polygraph tests to discount suspects where their own accounts (particularly in the case of Schmidt) were shaky at best. They failed to secure possession of Schmidt's Green Nova which may have proven to provide forensic evidence that Misty was in his vehicle.

Twenty-four years have elapsed since Misty's disappearance.

Her case remains unsolved.

RAILROAD KILLER

They called him the 'Railroad Killer.'

Angel Resendiz earned the nickname because of his penchant for committing his crimes near railroads, using the rail cars as his own personal get-away system.

Committing murder after murder, he was able to elude both American and Mexican authorities for over a decade.

EARLY LIFE

A birth certificate found by the FBI listed his date of birth as August 1st, 1960. He was born To Virginia de Maturino in the town of Izucar de Matomoros in the state of Puebla, Mexico. His mother has stated adamantly that the correct spelling of his surname is Recendis not Resendiz although the killer would have over fifty different aliases throughout his lifetime.

Angel had spent his childhood years with relatives and not with his immediate family. According to his mother, he was sexually abused by an uncle and other pedophiles in the town of Puebla. He would spend his youth roaming the streets, robbing, stealing and sniffing glue. Relatives would later testify that Resendiz was routinely beaten as a child, one time being "jumped" by several other youths who beat him so bad that he bled through his ears. Resendiz would leave home for months at a time then suddenly return mumbling about a coming religious apocalypse.

Legal trouble came early for Resendiz as he was caught trying to sneak into the Texas border at the age of sixteen. This would become the first of numerous run-ins with border patrol agents until he finally made it into the United States, making his way to St. Louis and finding work with a manufacturing company under an assumed name. He even registered to vote with his false identification.

In September of 1979, at the age of nineteen, Resendiz was arrested for assault and car theft in Miami. He was tried and sentenced to twenty-years in prison but was released after only six years and sent back to Mexico.

But he wouldn't stay there for long.

Through numerous attempts of trial and error, Resendiz had learned not only to game the system but to enter and exit the United States with minimal detection.

He learn to use the rail-cars...

AN "INVISIBLE" MAN

Resendiz became so skilled at crossing the border without detection that he began charging for his services. He began to make a living as a human smuggler, transporting Mexicans across the border for a fee.

Resendiz soon developed a reputation for his smuggling skills, often being seen as a 'go to' person in his Ciudad Juarez neighborhood called 'Patria.'

He would make weekly crossings over the border, being arrested only intermittently. He would then be deported back into his native land only to ping-pong back and forth.

Finally, Resendiz would serve prison terms for his crimes. He would be arrested in Texas for false identity and citizenship, getting a year and half worth of jail.

Upon release in 1987, he journeyed to New Orleans and was arrested for carrying a concealed weapon. He received another year and half worth of prison time until parole.

He then went back to his old haunts in St. Louis where he tried to defraud Social Security and receive illegal payments. He got caught and served a three year sentence.

Resendiz then decided small-time burglaries were his deal. He once again illegally crossed the border, journeyed to New Mexico and was caught burglarizing a home. He was imprisoned for eighteen months and upon release he broke into a Santa Fe rail yard, being captured yet again.

"They should have called Resendiz the boomerang man," forensic psychologist Frank Lizzo said. "He knew how to play the game and seemingly had no fear of the system. The system never punished him severely enough for him to stop his crimes, let alone stop crossing the border."

After his last recorded deportation, the killings began.

THE KILLING FIELDS

"He probably started killing somewhere in his late 20s," Douglas said. "He may have killed people like himself initially – males, transients...(he) became angry at the population at large. What America represents here is this wealthy country where he keeps getting kicked out...(he) just can't make ends meet. Coupled with these feelings, these inadequacies, fueled by the fact that he's known to take alcohol, take drugs, lowers his inhibitions now to go out and kill."

Angel's list of victims began in 1986. Continuing to bounce in and out of the United States, he shot a homeless woman and left her for dead in an abandoned farm house. He had met the acquaintance of the woman at a homeless shelter and they became friends. They would later take a trip on a motorcycle together when he felt that the woman disrespected him.

Resendiz would then take out his gun and blow her head off.

The woman allegedly had a boyfriend whom Resendiz shot and killed as well. He said that he dumped his body in a creek between San Antonio and Uvalde. This killing has never been verified aside from what Resendiz revealed to the police during his interrogation sessions.

Five years later, Resendiz would kill Michael White because he was a "homosexual." Resendiz would bludgeon White to death with a brick and leave him in front of an abandoned home.

These were seemingly warm-ups for the more brutal crimes to come which would also include rape.

"Sex seemed almost secondary," FBI profiler John Douglas said when apprised of Resendiz's crimes. "(He is) just a bungling crook ...very disorganized."

Douglas would later concede, however, that it was this disorganization that worked in his favor. Like a true drifter, Resendiz' whereabouts became as elusive as a rational thought in his head.

"When he hitches a ride on the freight train, he doesn't necessarily know where the train is going," Douglas said. "But when he gets off, having background as a burglar, he's able to scope out the area, do a little surveillance, make sure he breaks into the right house where there won't be anyone to give him a run for his money. He can enter a home complete with cutting glass and reaching in and undoing the locks."

"He'll look through the windows and see who's occupying it. The guy's only 5 foot-7, very small. In fact...the early weapons were primarily blunt-force trauma weapons, weapons of opportunity found at the scenes. He has to case them out, make sure he can put himself in a win-win situation."

Resendiz would also leave his weapon of choice up to chance. Whatever the home would have, a statue a mantle piece, a butcher knife, that would become the instrument of murder.

FLORIDA KILLINGS

On March 23rd, 1997, Jesse Howell would be found bludgeoned to death beside the railroad tracks in Ocala, Florida. He was nineteen years old.

"When we got there," Sheriff Patty Lumpkin said. "We see what appears to be a young male, in his late teens or early twenties. Blood around the head area. You could tell by looking at him that he was dead. The first thing I do is make sure that we've got our forensics people on the way, on the medical examiners on the way, and all the investigators that we have called out or either there or en route."

"When those types of things happen it might have been someone who had fallen off a train," Lt. Jeff Owens said. "Or someone who could have been struck by a train."

The authorities quickly ruled out an accident, however, as they examined the body.

"It didn't appear to be an accident," Lumpkin said. "Because if he had been hit by the train the trauma would have been much more extreme. I've seen some deaths from trains and the initial impact from the train would have done more harm to the body."

The forensic team did determine that Howell's body looked as if he were the victim of blunt force trauma.

"We did see a baseball type of cap," forensic scientist Michael Dunn said. "It appeared to have blood on the inside surface of he bill. In addition, there was a pair of wire rimmed eye glasses and one of the eye pieces was missing, one of the lenses was out. This didn't look good either. As we moved closer, we saw that the victim had been dragged to that spot using just the blue jean material around the cuff (of his pants)."

Near the body, they found a brass and rubber coupling. This device was used to link one train car to another. It could also be used as a clubbing weapon.

"It had what appeared to be blood on it (the coupling)," Dunn recalled.

Howell still had jewelry on his person. He wore a gold cross necklace, a watch and a small amount of cash in his pocket. The police ruled out robbery as a motive.

The police did not identify Howell's body right off the bat. They did find a money wire receipt where some money had been wired from Illinois to Florida. The name on the receipt was of a woman named "Wendy."

Police tracked the money transfer to its point of origin which was all the way in Woodstock, Illinois.

Coincidentally, the authorities there were investigating the disappearance of Wendy Von Huben.

Wendy was missing alongside her boyfriend, the nineteen year old Jesse Howell.

"They advised me that they were investigating a John Doe," Woodstock Detective Kurt Rosenquest recalled. "Unidentified male."

Rosenquest then followed up with the investigating team in Florida, sending them the fingerprints and pictures of Jesse Howell.

The Ocala police would then positively identify Howell.

Jesse had met Wendy only months earlier. They had secretly planned to marry and went on a road trip with another couple.

The other couple, however, grew tired of Jesse and Wendy's constant bickering. They demanded to be let out of the car and left. Jesse and Wendy continued into Ocala, Florida where they ran out of money.

Wendy would call her parents in Illinois who would then transfer her $200 via Western Union. The couple would collect the $200 but would not return home.

"We checked Greyhounds," Rosenquest said. "Nobody matching their description ordered buses or train tickets back to the Woodstock area."

Tears were shed as Rosenquest informed Howell's parents that their teen son had been murdered. The investigative team then turned their attention to the disappearance of Wendy.

They held out hope because there were issues between her and Jesse, thinking that perhaps she simply ran off to be by herself.

Police scoured the surrounding areas and used helicopters in all directions around the railroad tracks.

They would find nothing. There was no DNA left behind on Jesse Howell's body either.

Papers and fliers with Wendy Von Huben's information was distributed all throughout Florida up through Illinois.

Authorities also began interviewing the transient population that lived along the railroad tracks.

Two and a half months later, however, Wendy's parents would receive a phone call.

"The phone rang," Rosenquest recalled. "Wendy's father answered the phone. The girl was crying. She said 'I'm sorry. I love you.'"

She would tell the father she was two hours away from Woodstock at a gas station. The father asked for the phone number on the pay phone she was calling from and she said that there wasn't any before hanging up.

The police were not certain that the phone call came from Wendy so they immediately headed out to the gas station where they believe the call took place.

Police tracked down the surveillance video of the gas station. On the video, a woman that physically resembled Wendy entered the gas station.

The phone records, however, revealed that the call did not come from the gas station where the surveillance video revealed a woman who allegedly was Wendy. It came from another gas station where there were fliers posted of Wendy.

Someone had played a cruel hoax as Wendy's parents had added their home number to the fliers

ONE-LEGGED BOB AND A CHANCE DISCOVERY

A year went by without any sign of Wendy.

There was some ray of hope, however, as the railroad authorities called the Ocala police and informed them that the received information from a member of one of the homeless camps. They had a man in custody named "One Legged Bob" who was traveling with a girl and may be responsible for the murder of her previous boyfriend.

"'One Legged Bob' was your typical homeless person," Owens said. "Kinda scruffy. Hadn't shaved in a few days. He had a prosthetic leg that helped him get around. For someone who you might consider crippled, he was far from crippled."

Owens would spend the next eight hours interviewing the only lead he had, a one legged homeless man.

After the grueling interrogation, Owens realized that he had the wrong suspect.

By sheer chance, however, Patty Lumpkin heard about someone they dubbed the "Railroad Killer" during a class she was taking at the FBI.

"They called him the Railway Killer," Lumpkin recalled. "The Angel of Death. He was killing people. Leaving them near the railroad or he was killing them at homes or locations that were close to the railroad.

The FBI knew the Railway Killer as Angel Resendiz.

"We knew that Angel Resendiz was a person that rode the rails across the country," FBI Agent Mark Young said. "We were worried where he'd wind up next. So we decided to make him a top ten fugitive. Maybe the millions of eyes of the public would tell us something."

The strategy worked.

"He was one of the most vile, evil persons that I had ever dealt with," Young said. "It was like every time you turn around there's another murder."

Owens and Lumpkin hoped to talk to Resendiz to query him about Jesse Howell's murder and Wendy Von Huben's disappearance.

"The attorneys representing him at the time in Texas stopped us," Owens said. "They wanted to protect their client from talking. Any defense attorney who represents a criminal will generally tell the person to stop talking to law enforcement."

Resendiz was placed on death row and Texas had a fast execution rate. The two detectives worried that they would lose their chance to interview Resendiz and connect him to the crimes in Ocala.

Owens and Lumpkin decided to mail Resendiz a letter, respectfully asking him if they could interview him. The letter was written in a formal manner and even addressed him as "Senor."

To their surprise, Resendiz responded back and granted them an interview regarding his involvement in Jesse's killing and Wendy's disappearance.

During their meeting, Resendiz was quick to admit that he had killed Jesse. The detectives deliberately withheld information about the killing, holding back details that only the killer would know. But when Resendiz described using a brake coupling from one of the trains, they knew they had their killer.

But they needed to find out what happened to Wendy.

In a follow-up letter, they promised him immunity from prosecution if he agreed to talk. It was a moot point by then as he was already on death row but the detectives still needed permission from Wendy's family to go through with the interview.

In order to receive some sense of closure, the family agreed to the immunity.

"When we get to the prison," Lumpkin said. "We see him coming down the hallway. He (Resendiz) has a waist belt on. It's an electric shock belt and he's chained to the belt. He's just a mild-mannered person but remember that a psychopath or a sociopath doesn't have any feeling. I mean he had dead eyes. He had no feeling in that body. He didn't care about anything."

Resendiz would reveal that he was heading south for work when the train stopped and he spotted Jesse getting off the train for a smoke.

"Resendiz told us that he killed Jesse with a piece of the train coupling," Lumpkin said. "And Wendy was asleep on the train when this took place. And then when they went down the road further somehow he talked Wendy into getting off the train."

Resendiz then raped and strangled Wendy to death.

Resendiz drew a map of where had left Wendy's

body. He described burying her in a shallow grave near a canopy of trees. Resendiz would remember that she had a book in a back pack and an army style jacket that he used to cover her fresh grave.

Police would return to the site and were able to locate where he buried Wendy's body. Almost three years after the murder, everything the killer described was still there. The book. The jacket.

And Wendy's body.

"When Wendy ran away she had a small engagement ring," Owen said. "And she had a Winnie the Pooh wristwatch.

The detective would bring those items back to Wendy's parents.

KENTUCKY RAILROAD MURDER

In August of 1997, Resendiz would make his way from Ocala, Florida to Lexington, Kentucky. It was there he would stalk two young college students.

Holly Dunn was a 20-year old junior at the University of Kentucky and it was there she met Christopher Maier.

"Chris Maier was my very good friend," Dunn recalled. "He was just the nicest, kindest man. We decided that we wanted to be more than friends then we started dating. We dated for about three months."

"Chris and I were attending a party. We decided that the party wasn't very fun so we went to go talk a walk by the railroad tracks. We sat down and talked for awhile and when we got up to leave a man came out from behind an electrical box. He had a weapon that he used on Chris. It was some sort of ice pick or screw driver. Something sharp. I guess our immediate thought was he's going to rob us. That's when we realize he wants money we start thinking 'okay, well, you could have our credit card, you can have our ATM card, you can have our car.' Then he started tying up Chris' hands behind his back. And then he came over to me and he took off my belt and that's when I started thinking he doesn't want to rob us."

After tying up Holly, Resendiz then pulled Chris by the shirt across the railroad tracks and into a ditch.

Holly would follow on her knees, pleading for him to stop whatever he was about to do.

"Lie down," Resendiz said, his voice soft but menacing.

"Everything is going to be okay," Christopher said to Holly as Resendiz dragged him into the ditch.

"Shut up!" Resendiz commanded as he gagged Christopher with a sock.

Resendiz then walked off into the darkness. The frightened couple did not know what the psychopath had planned.

"Then he comes with this rock," Holly recalled.

"There was no warning, he drops this rock on Chris' head. I'm just thinking 'what just happened?' I don't even know what just happened."

"You don't have to worry about him anymore," Resendiz said to Holly as he got on top of her.

"I went into survival mode, I'm thinking, I mean he's gonna kill me. I may as well fight. I'm gonna fight. He unties my feet and climbs on top of me. I start to kick and scream and hit him but he held that knife or ice pick (to my throat) and said 'look how easily I could kill you.' I stopped everything and then he raped me."

"I memorized his face," Dunn said. "I stared at him and memorized, he had a tattoo on his arm, I was thinking if you have any scars I'm gonna remember your scars, I'm gonna remember your face,I'm not gonna forget it because if I live through this I will get you."

Resendiz completed the sexual assault of Dunn before smashing her head with a rock.

"He hit me five or six times in my face," Dunn recalled. "I think I put my hand up and then I turned over and then he hit me five or six times in the back of my head. He hit me hard. He was trying to kill me. I think I laid there and he thought I was dead."

Resendiz did think she was did as he threw the rock down and ran away from the crime scene.

Holly would suffer severe facial trauma but miraculously survived the attack.

"I had a broken jaw," Dunn said. "Broken eye socket and cuts on the back of my head that they had to staple shut and then I had cuts on my face."

She woke up in a Kentucky hospital, surrounded by family members.

"Everyone was told not to talk about Chris to me. I just said 'Chris is dead, isn't he?' And my Dad actually is the one I said that to and he was like 'yes, he died.'"

TEXAS TERROR

Resendiz would travel to Texas via train and in October of 1988 he flopped down in Hughes Springs. He would enter the home of 87-year old Leafie Mason, attacking the woman with an iron and killing her.

Two months later, Resendiz would sneak into the home of Dr. Claudia Benton, a thirty-nine year old medical researcher who lived in a suburb of Houston near the railroad tracks.

Again, it was a case of a home being to close to the train tracks. The train would provide the perfect cover for the sneaky Resendiz as he realized that the sound of the rail-car racing by would allow him to break in homes without being heard.

He applied the same technique with Benton, breaking into her home, raping then killing her.

Police would find the doctor face down on the floor. Her bedroom soaked in blood, ransacked for any valuables.

He head had been covered in a plastic bag while her body had been covered in a blanket.

"It appears that she (Claudia Benton) was sleeping," recalled Ken Macha, former police sergeant. "He was able to get in and picked up a bronze statuette from the mantle in the living room. He was relentless in beating her. The skull fractures themselves would have been enough to kill her. She was then stabbed in the back with a very large butcher knife."

"Resendiz was brutal, sadistic," said former West University police chief Gary Brye.

Fingerprints and DNA evidence would link Resendiz to the crime.

The problem was they could catch the man that Texas Ranger Drew Carter referred to as "a walking, breathing form of evil."

EVADING POLICE

Seven months later, Resendiz would continue to avoid capture. He remained in Texas, riding the rail cars until coming into the town of Weimar. He would break into the home of Pastor Norman "Skip" Sirnic and his wife Karen. Resendiz smashed a jack hammer into both of their heads, killing them instantly. He would then rape the body of Karen postmortem.

"He would watch these places," prosecuting attorney Devin Anderson said. "He would watch them, wait for them to go to sleep, get in their house and he would strike them before they would even wake up. I thought we have got to catch this guy."

The DNA found at the scene of the Sirnic murders would match those left on Benton. The FBI then realized they had a highly mobile serial killer on the loose...someone who could kill in one town then appear in another town miles away and kill again.

Resendiz was also smart. He would constantly alter his appearance. He'd shave his head. Then his mustache. He'd be clean shaven one week. Unkempt the next. He would wear glasses one week. No glasses the next.

Authorities could not get an accurate description of him other than the fact that he was small.

Resendiz was also able to take advantage of the lack of a coordinated computer system that gave law enforcement the ability to cross-check fugitives. After the Sirnic murders, Border Patrol had encountered Resendiz near the El Paso border but did not find him on the wanted list.

They then deported him back to Mexico.

Within 48 hours, Resendiz was back across the border to resume his killing spree.

"Our computers told us that he was nothing of lookout material," said C.G. Almengor, a supervisor at the border. "We really wish he had been in the system so we could have caught him."

Resendiz would be deported no less than seventeen times over the course of his rampage. At no point did authorities make the connection because of his changing appearance, use of different aliases and the lack of a connected system to document illegals trying to come across the border.

A PREFERENCE FOR TEXAS

Noemi Dominguez was a graduate of Rice University who had just recently quit her job as an elementary school teacher to pursue a master's degree.

She was described as "the sweetest, nicest teacher – a darling who went the extra mile."

Fueled by hate, Resendiz would break into Noemi's home and rape her before killing her with a pick ax. He then stole her car and drove to Schulenberg, Texas where he would kill Josephine Konvicka with the same pick ax.

He would leave the weapon embedded in Konvicka's head as well as leave his fingerprints all over the home. He was more than just sloppy, he was getting cocky. He left a newspaper article that described his crimes as well as a toy train…a reference to his nickname as the "Railroad Killer."

Resendiz was also meticulous in approaching his victims.

"He undid the light in her (Noemi's) car," Anderson said. "So when he opened the door it wouldn't come on. That's who were were dealing with. Someone who really knew how to sneak around. Who really knew how to avoid detection."

"He kept killing people. He would not stop. In his mode of transportation, using the railroads was brilliant because they couldn't be monitored. I mean there's thousands of trains and millions of miles of tracks all over the United States."

"I felt hopeless at the time. Because if you're willing to sleep in a train or you're willing to sleep in a field, you can stay lost for a long, long time and I didn't think we were ever going to catch him."

Later that month, Resendiz had journeyed to Illinois, reaching the town of Gorham. He would break into the home of 80-year old George Morber and his daughter Carolyn Frederick. Resendiz would tie Morber to a chair and shoot him in the back of the head with a shotgun. He then raped Carolyn and smashed the shotgun across her head with such force that the weapon broke in half.

Both Morber and Frederick would die from their injuries.

The FBI placed him on their Top Ten list.

They then recruited his common-law wife, Julietta Reyes, and brought her into Houston for questioning from her hometown of Rodeo, Mexico.

Reyes complied with police requests, turning over over ninety-three pieces of jewelry that her husband had mailed to her from the U.S.

Relatives of Noemi Dominguez claimed thirteen pieces. George Benton was able to identify some pieces of jewelry as belonging to his wife as well.

Police would then locate Resendiz's half-sister, Manuela Karkiewicz, who lived in New Mexico. Initially, she refused to cooperate. She worried that the FBI or the police would kill her brother. But Carter convinced her to talk Resendiz into giving himself up.

The FBI knew that Resendiz had made his way back to Mexico after the murders in Illinois and was hiding in his hometown neighborhood of Patria.

Carter was able to get a rapport with Manuela. He convinced her that Resendiz would receive "personal safety while in jail, regular visiting rights for his family and a psychological evaluation."

"I came away with the impression that they (Resendiz' family) definitely had an understanding of right and wrong ... and knew now that what Maturino Resendiz was accused of doing was heinous and wrong ... ," Carter said. "Manuela, especially, came across as a woman of strong faith. There was a very deep emotional strain and burden placed on her in this investigation. She had to make some very difficult choices that impacted her and her family. And, in the end, her actions alone speak to her character."

Carter spent weeks talking to Manuela who in turn "worked a miracle."

They got the serial killer to surrender.

On July 12th, Manuela would receive a fax from the district attorney's office in Harris County which formalized everything that Texas Ranger Carter had promised.

The word passed from Manuela to another relative who acted as a go-between with Resendiz. The relative than came back later that evening and said that Resendiz would surrender in the morning at 9 a.m.

Texas Ranger Drew Carter would accompany Manuela and a spiritual adviser to meet with Resendiz on a bridge that connected El Paso, Texas to Ciudad Juarez.

"When I saw that face there was a little bit of excitement there because I finally said, 'This is going to happen,'" Carter recalled as he remembered Resendiz appearing on the bridge with his dirty jeans, muddy boots and blank facial expression. "He stuck out his hand, I stuck out my hand, and we shook hands."

Resendiz would then surrender to the Texas Ranger.

DEATH PENALTY

Resendiz' attorneys knew that their only hope would be an insanity defense. The Mexican government also got involved, lobbying authorities to spare Resendiz the death penalty

"Insanity was the logical defense because no one wants to believe that there is someone out there who would do things like that," Anderson said. "That was the thing that worried me the most about the case was that jurors would just throw up their hands and say nobody in their right mind could do what he does."

"The thing about what a life sentence with Resendiz would have been, he would have enjoyed it. I mean he would have had pen pals. He would have given interviews if they let him, I mean he would have loved it. And I knew that. And he didn't deserve to live after what he did just didn't. He caused so much pain, so much heartache and so much terror, that's what the whole focus of the trial had to be."

George Benton, the husband of Claudia, would vehemently criticize the Mexican government who support his appeals and domestic opposition to the death penalty.

"(He)looked like a man and walked like a man. But what lived within that skin was not a human being."

"He was small," Anderson said when she first saw Resendiz in the courtroom. "Maybe five- foot five. His forearms though, were roped with muscles. He was scary. Even though he was small you could feel he was dangerous. He looked like a wild animal who'd been caught."

Resendiz looked "timid" in the courtroom and spoke of himself in religious riddles. He claimed he was Jewish and didn't seem effected when he was informed that the prosecution was aiming for the death penalty.

"I don't believe in death," Resendiz, said. "I know the body is going to go to waste. But me, as a person, I'm eternal. I'm going to be alive forever."

The defense said that Resendiz' crimes were caused by head injuries, drug abuse and a family history of mental illness. He has a delusional perception of the world as he believes that he can cause earthquakes, floods, and explosions and that God told him to kill his victims whom they believed to be evil.

He made a living stealing things from his victims and having his wife sell them in Mexico. "That was his job," Anderson said. "And for recreation it was killing the people who lived in the house."

"He was a very intelligent person who worked the system and knew exactly what kinds of things to say to get that defense to work."

The jury, however, would find Resendiz guilty after one hour and forty-five minutes of deliberation.

He was sentenced to die via lethal injection.

"He made it very clear during my conversation with him that he deserves to die," Owens said.

"I want to ask if it is in your heart to forgive me," Resendiz said in his final words. "You don't have to. I know I allowed the devil to rule my life. I just ask you to forgive me and ask the Lord to forgive me for allowing the devil to deceive me. I thank God for having patience with me. I don't deserve to cause you pain. You did not deserve this. I deserve what I am getting."

Resendiz then prayed in Hebrew and Spanish before drawing his final breath.

MISSING MADELEINE

MARY CHILDRESS

Madeleine McCann, a young child of three years old, was visiting the popular Portuguese resort town of Praia da Luiz along with her parents and younger siblings, as well as a group of her parents' close friends, when she went missing on the night of May 3rd. Madeleine's disappearance became an international sensation and various police departments in both Portugal and the United Kingdom, as well as Madeleine's parents, would conduct independent investigations into her disappearance and the circumstances surrounding that night.

Background

Madeleine Beth McCann was born on May 12th, 2003 to Gerry and Kate McCann in the small town of Leicester, in the United Kingdom, before moving to Rothley in Leicestershire as a young child. Both Gerry and Kate McCann were both practicing physicians and prominent members of the local Roman Catholic community, and had a total of three young children at the time of Madeleine's disappearance, Madeleine as well as two younger siblings: a twin boy and girl.

The entire McCann family set out for the popular Portuguese resort town of Praia da Luz (referred to as "little Britain" because of the large amount of British vacationers who frequented the town) on Saturday, April 28th for a family vacation with seven other adults and five additional children.

The McCanns rented a small apartment owned by a retired British schoolteacher through a private vacation company. The unit, a two-bedroom ground level apartment in the resort's Waterside Village, was next door to several of their friends' rented apartments. The unit was accessible from two locations: a sliding glass patio door and a front door facing the popular Ocean Club. The room's sliding glass door and patio overlooked the Ocean Club's facilities, including the tapas bar that Madeleine's parents would dine at the night of her disappearance.

The nine adults who made up the party included the McCann parents, Russell O'Brien, Matthew Oldfield and his spouse, Rachael Oldfield, Dianne Webster, David Payne, Fiona Payne, and Jane Tanner and her significant other. These friends would later be referred to as the "Tapas Seven," after the tapas bar that they were dining at the night of Madeleine's disappearance.

Night of Disappearance

During the daytime on May 3rd, the group's last night at the resort, the children spent the morning playing at the resort's Kids' Club, also eating lunch with their parents and spending a couple of hours at the children's pool. The last known photo of Madeleine was taken that afternoon by Kate McCann, showing the young girl sitting by the pool next to her father and sister.

On the night of Madeleine's disappearance, her mother put Madeleine and her siblings down for bed around 7:00pm, wearing her favorite Marks and Spencer's Eeyore pajamas. At 8:30pm, the group of nine adults decided to have dinner and drinks at the nearby tapas bar, located just 160 feet away from the hotel rooms that the children were staying in. Kate McCann described the tapas bar as being located directly across the pool from the children's room and being just a 30-second walk away.

The group of adults had requested a table on the patio which overlooked their children's rooms, so that the parents could have peace of mind while dining. Kate McCann has stated that a resort staff member left a note in the message book in the swimming pool area stating that the group of adults was requesting a specific table so that they would have a view of the hotel rooms in which their children were staying in. She has indicated that she believes the kidnapper saw this note earlier in the day and decided to kidnap her Madeleine upon realizing that the children were to be left unguarded at night.

The McCanns stated that the group of adults agreed to check on the children every 30 minutes, with each adult taking a different shift and helping to check on the eight children located in several different rooms. Because the McCann's patio doors could only be unlocked from the inside, the McCanns left the curtain down and doors closed, but left the patio door unlocked. This is presumably how the kidnapper was able to enter the room. It should be noted that the parents also set up a child-safety gate at both the top of the patio stairs and at the bottom, making it extremely unlikely that Madeleine wandered out of the room.

Gerry McCann performed the first check on his children at 9:05pm, and he reported the children as sleeping safely and soundly. However, he did notice that the children's bedroom door, which he had left open just an inch or two, was nearly wide open when he performed his check on the children. This was the last time that either of the parents would see Madeleine.

Matthew Oldfield, a friend of the McCanns and member of the Tapas Seven, volunteers to check on all of the children at 9:30pm (his children were sleeping in the room next door). When he enters the McCann's room, he notices that the children's bedroom door was wide open. However, he states that upon hearing no noises, he left the apartment without physically looking inside of the children's room. He later states that he did not notice whether there was a draft or whether the bedroom window was open. The fact that he volunteered to check on the children and his claim that he did not actually look in the room caused him to be viewed as a primary suspect by the local police department.

Roughly thirty minutes later, at 10:00pm, Kate McCann walks back to her hotel room to check on her children. Kate stated that she entered the apartment through the patio door and immediately noticed that the children's bedroom door was completely open. Noticing nothing amiss and hearing no noises, Kate attempted to close the bedroom door without looking inside. However, the door closed rapidly and loudly, as if there was a strong draft pulling the door closed.

When Kate reopened the door to see where the draft was coming from, she noticed that the children's window and shutter were both open and that Madeleine was missing from her bed. The young girl's blanket and favorite stuffed toy were still lying on the bed, but her daughter was nowhere to be seen. After frantically searching the apartment for Madeleine, Kate began running back towards the restaurant screaming that her daughter had been taken.

Upon hearing from Kate, Gerry McCann asked Matthew Oldfield to go to the hotel lobby and contact the police. The hotel staff called the local police department at 10:30am and began mobilizing their staff and willing guests to help in the search for young Madeleine. The combined 60 hotel staff members and guests searched for Madeleine until 4:30am, screaming her name throughout the resort.

Police Arrival

At approximately 11:10pm, two officers from the national military police arrive to investigate the missing child report. After conducting a brief search of the resort, they contact the local police force to assist with the search. Two officers from the local police force arrive at 11:20pm to begin assisting with the search and to investigate the hotel room. Later that morning, both patrol dogs and search and rescue dogs were brought in to assist with the search for Madeleine. A road block was not put into place until 10:00am that morning.

      The initial police response consisted of a variety of mistakes and oversights that prevented crucial evidence from being gathered. First of all, more than twenty different people were allowed to enter the apartment before it was closed off for investigation, potentially corrupting a wide range of evidence. In addition, although police officers did place "Do Not Enter" crime scene tape over the doorway to the children's room at 3:00am, they did not secure the apartment itself from people entering it. In addition, although police did not allow tourists to stay in the apartment for a full month after Madeleine's disappearance, tourists were again allowed to stay in the apartment for several months until it was closed off to the public again in August 2007 for additional forensic testing and analysis.

      Police officers also allowed a fairly substantial crowd of people to congregate on the patio, directly outside of the children's window. It is thought that a great deal of forensic evidence was corrupted as a result of this. Additionally, the officer responsible for dusting the children's window and gathering fingerprint evidence did so without using gloves, possibly corrupting yet another set of evidence.

      Furthermore, during the manhunt for Madeleine, several additional mistakes were made. The police did not provide a description of Madeleine or pictures of the young girl to the border police or coast guard force until several hours after her disappearance. Roadblocks were also not put into place until 10:00am that morning, meaning that Madeleine could have been in another country by the time key law enforcement figures even began to search for her. Lastly, Interpol, the global anti-crime organization, did not issue an alert about her disappearance for a full five days after she was reported as missing, allowing her kidnappers crucial time to escape and transport her out of the country or even out of the continent.

Child Sightings

Jane Tanner
Jane Tanner, one of the "Tapas Seven," reported seeing a man carrying a child through the resort complex the night of the disappearance. Jane left the tapas bar at 9:00pm to personally check on her own children in their nearby hotel room and reported passing Madeleine's father, on his way back from checking on his own children, during her walk to the hotel room.

While Jane claimed to have seen Gerry McCann on her way to check on her own children, both Gerry and an English vacationer that he stopped to chat with, do not remember seeing her pass by on the very narrow street. This discrepancy later cast doubt on her story and led to Portuguese authorities accusing her of inventing the story.

At approximately 9:10pm, Jane reported that she saw a man and a child cross the street at *Rua Dr Francisco Gentil Martins* and *Rua Dr Agostinho da Silva* heading away from the Ocean Club, towards the east. She described the man looking like a local and as carrying a barefoot child across the intersection. The man was described as being of Mediterranean appearance, dark-haired, roughly 5' 7" tall, and wearing khakis with a dark jacket. The child was seen wearing light-colored pink pajamas with floral patterns. Although Jane reported this sighting to the local police department soon after Madeleine was discovered missing, the police did not release any information on this possible suspect until some three weeks later, on May 25th.

Despite Jane's seemingly important sighting, a later investigation by Scotland Yard would rule out this individual as a suspect. British police were able to identify the man as a vacationer staying in the same resort as the McCanns. He was carrying his daughter back to their hotel room after picking her up from a play hour for children at the resort. It would later be confirmed that his daughter was wearing light-pink pajamas with floral prints that night.

Martin and Mary Smith
Two other vacationers staying at the resort reporting seeing a man carrying a young child the night of Madeleine's disappearance. Martin and Mary Smith reported seeing a man walking down Rua da Escola Primaria, towards Rua 25 de Abril and away from the resort, at approximately 10:00pm that night. The man was sighted just 500 yards from the McCann's apartment.

The Smiths stated that the man did not look like a tourist and that he did not seem comfortable interacting with the child in his arms. The man was described as being in his mid-30s, approximately 5' 8", with short brown hair and khakis on. The child was described as being three or four years old, with blond hair and light colored pajamas. The young girl was also barefoot.

Those Present at Time of Disappearance

The McCanns were accompanied by a group of

seven adults and five children on their vacation to Praia da Luz. All seven adults were present at the tapas bar for at least part of the night. Jane Tanner, an English marketing executive, and her partner Russell O'Brien were staying in one room with their two children. Fiona and David Payne, as well as Fiona's mother, Dianne Webster, and their two children were staying in another room. Lastly, Matthew Oldfield and his wife, Rachael Oldfield, were staying in the last room along with their young daughter.

Timeline

7:00pm - Gerry and Kate McCann put their three children to bed. The children are all sleeping in the bedroom closest to the front door.

8:30pm - Gerry and Kate McCann leave the hotel to meet their friends at the resort's tapas bar, located just 160 feet from the hotel room and in sight of the patio door. The parents reportedly leave the patio door unlocked, but the door closed and the curtains drawn.

9:05pm - Gerry McCann checks on the children in their room. He reports that the children were sleeping safe and sound. He stops to speak with another tourist for a few minutes on his was back to the tapas bar.
9:10pm - Jane Tanner recalls seeing Gerry speaking with the English tourist on the street leading back to the tapas bar. Neither man recalls seeing Jane Tanner, which casts doubt on her story given how narrow the street was. Tanner notices a man crossing the street with a child in his arms. This sighting is later ruled out by Scotland Yard detectives.

9:30pm - Matthew Oldfield, a member of the Tapas Seven, visits the McCann's room to check on the children.

He notices that the bedroom door is wide open, but upon hearing no noise, he does not go far enough into the apartment to see whether Madeleine is in bed. He does not recall the bedroom window being open at this time.

10:00pm - Martin and Mary Smith, two tourists staying in the same resort, recall seeing a man carrying a barefoot child down the street, away from the resort.

10:00pm - Kate McCann visits the hotel room to check on her children. She entered the apartment through the patio doors and noticed that the bedroom door was wide open and then sees that the window is open as well. She notices that Madeleine is missing and, after performing a quick check of the entire apartment, runs back to the restaurant screaming that her daughter is missing.

10:10pm - Gerry McCann asks the resort to call the police and report Madeleine as missing.

10:30pm - The hotel begins treating Madeleine's disappearance as a missing childrens case. The hotel mobilizes sixty staff members and guests to search the entire resort complex for Madeleine. Reportedly, guests could hear Madeleine's name being screamed out until 4:30am that morning.

11:10pm - Two officers from the Guarda Nacional Republicana, essentially the country's military police, arrive at the resort to conduct a search for Madeleine. After conducting a quick search, they contact the local criminal police department for assistance.

11:20pm - Two officers from the Policia Judiciaria, the local police department, arrive to assist with the search and investigate the McCann's hotel room for clues.

2:00am - Two patrol dogs arrive at the resort to assist with the search for Madeleine.

8:00am - Four search and rescue dogs arrive at the resort to search for Madeleine. Local police officers are called in from vacation and during their days off to assist with the search. They begin searching local waterways, wells, and sewers.

10:00am - Police setup road blocks to prevent the abductor from leaving with the child. The local police department did not ask for photos of cars seen leaving the area at the time of Madeleine's disappearance.

Portuguese Investigation

Portuguese investigators interviewed several witnesses who reported seeing a group of two strange men in the area of the McCann's apartment the morning of the abduction, as well as several days earlier. On the day of Madeleine's disappearance, two men were spotted visiting the area surrounding the McCann's apartment, with one man being spotted on the actual street. The two men, who were visiting the area from 3:30 to 5:30pm the evening of Madeleine's disappearance, said that they were visiting tourist rooms in order to collect donations for a local orphanage. Investigators from Scotland Yard would later say that they believed the two men were casing the street and planning their abduction.

Witnesses would also report seeing several blond-haired men around the McCann's apartment in the days leading up to Madeleine's disappearance. Earlier in the day on May 3rd, a man was seen walking through a gate near their apartment, attempting to close the gate door quietly and without being noticed. Later that evening, at least one blond man was seen standing near the McCann's room at 4:00pm and again at 6:00pm.

At 11:00pm that night, two blond men were seen speaking to each other in loud voices, but reportedly lowered their voices and hurried off upon noticing that they were being observed. Witnesses also reported seeing a man leaning against a wall next to the McCann's apartment the day before the disappearance, with a white unmarked van parked next to the apartment. All in all, several witnesses report seeing suspicious men near the McCann's apartment in the days leading up to Madeleine's disappearance, and report seeing the men staring at or watching the McCann's apartment.

Parents' Reaction

In May 2007, Gerry and Kate McCann set up a private fund to investigate the disappearance of their daughter, calling the organization *Madeleine's Fund: Leaving No Stone Unturned*. Over $2.6 million was raised to help in the search for their daughter, and the British publication *News of the World* offered a $1.5 million reward for information leading to her return or conclusively proving her fate. Despite the creation of the fund, the McCanns were accused of using the money to pay for their mortgage payment on at least two occasions. The fund has yet to make any progress on ascertaining the fate of Madeleine McCann.

Scotland Yard Investigation

In May 2011, Scotland Yard launched its own investigation of Madeleine's disappearance, assigning a team of 29 police officers to the case, along with eight civilian consultants. Scotland Yard investigators eventually settled on the theory that Madeleine had been taken during a burglary gone wrong. Because there had been a rapid increase in the volume of burglaries in that area in the months preceding Madeleine's disappearance (including cases where the burglars had robbed houses on the McCann's block by entering through the window), they theorized that burglars had kidnapped Madeleine after she woke up and saw their faces during the middle of their robbery attempt.

The British investigators also questioned a group of manual laborers who were working out of a white van in that area at the time of Madeleine's disappearance, as well as two convicted child molesters who were reportedly in that general area during that timeframe. However, despite the developments of new leads in the case, British investigators were never able to determine who actually kidnapped Madeleine.

Suspects

Robert Murat
The first suspect identified by Portuguese police was Robert Murat, a British-Portuguese consultant who lived with his mother just 150 yards away from the location where Jane Tanner spotted a man carrying a barefoot child. Three separate members of the McCann's party later stated that they saw Murat near the resort of the evening of May 3rd, although both Murat and his mother told police that he was at home all-evening long.

Police conducted a thorough investigation of Robert Murat and his possessions, going so far as to conduct a forensic analysis on his computer, phone, and video camera, and even searching his home and property with police sniffer dogs and ground-penetrating radar. Despite the police investigation of Murat and his property, he was cleared on July 21, 2008, when the Portuguese justice department closed the case. However, he was questioned again in 2014 by Portuguese police on behalf of Scotland Yard once the case was re-opened.

Gerry and Kate McCann
While Madeleine's parents were initially viewed with sympathy by the media and general public, they soon became suspects in the case. On June 6th, 2007, a German journalist asked the McCanns if they were involved in the daughter's disappearance during a public press conference. Later that month, local Portuguese paper began writing a series of accusatory articles about the McCanns and their role in their daughter's disappearance.

One of the factors that led to so much speculation about the McCanns and their potential role in their daughter's disappearance was the fact that their initial interview with local police was conducted using a translator. The police investigators would ask a question in Portuguese and then have the translator ask the question in English. The McCanns and their friends would then answer the question in English, which was then translated into Portuguese for the police. Finally, the police then typed up the statement provided by the McCanns and members of the Tapas Seven in Portuguese, before verbally reading the statement back to them in English and asking them to sign the document. This constant translation may have contributed to the discrepancies contained in the statements of all those present that night.

There were several inconsistencies in the McCann's statements. For instance, both parents initially said that they entered the apartment through the locked front door when the checked on their children. However, they would later state that they entered the patio doors at the back of the apartment. In addition, the parents alternatively stated that the patio door was both locked and unlocked that night, casting doubt on their statements. Gerry McCann later told a British newspaper that they had used the front door to check on their children earlier in the vacation, but that they started using the patio door because the front door was next to the children's room and woke them up on their bi-hourly check-ins.

The McCanns also provided contradictory statements on the room's exterior shutter. While Kate McCann told police that the shutter was closed when she put the children to bed at 7:00pm, she claimed that the shutter and window were both open when she discovered that Madeleine was missing. Gerry McCann told police that he closed the shutter after discovering that Madeleine was gone. He also said that, after investigating the shutter from outside the apartment, he noticed that it could be opened from outside. However, the local police said that the shutter was incapable of being opened from the outside and that the lack of evidence of forceful entry ruled out the theory that the abductors had entered through the window.

This important detail led the local Policia Judiciaria to concluded that Madeleine had never been abducted and that the McCanns had made up the story to hide some wrongdoing committed by the parents, even theorizing that Madeleine had actually died in an accident and that the McCann had created the abduction story to shield themselves from scrutiny.

After suspicions about Gerry and Kate were made public, two police sniffing dogs were brought in by Mark Harrison, a national search specialist for the British National

Policing Improvement Agency, to conduct an investigation of the apartment, as well as items left by the McCanns and their rental car at the time of Madeleine's disappearance. The two dogs were taken throughout the entire resort, including inside of the McCann's apartment; the dogs alerted their handlers that they smelled signs of Madeleine at the apartment, but did not alert their handlers anywhere else in the resort.

Additionally, the dogs also alerted their handlers of a clue directly behind the couch in the apartment, as well as under the veranda of the bedroom that Gerry and Kate were sleeping in at the time of Madeleine's disappearance. Furthermore, upon additional investigation the cadaver dog alerted its handler when walked around the McCann's rental car, particularly around the outside of the car and inside the trunk of the car. However, the Sunday Times would later say that footage of this investigation clearly showed the dog's handler manipulating the dog and encouraging it to signal a find when passing by those locations.

DNA Analysis

On August 8th, 2007, DNA samples from the McCann's rental car were sent to the Forensic Science Service in Birmingham, England, for testing. The low copy number DNA analysis, which is known for its lack of accuracy and inability to draw conclusive results, demonstrated that 15 out of 19 of Madeleine's DNA pieces were found in areas where the cadaver dogs had signified Madeleine had been, both in the apartment and in the McCann's rental car.

Once Portuguese authorities were notified of the results of this DNA test, they officially abandoned the abduction hypothesis and marked Madeleine's parents as official suspects in the case. They even offered the McCanns a plea deal: they would receive a two-year sentence or less if they admitted that Madeleine had died in an accident and that Kate had hidden the body out of fear of being arrested. Gerry McCann cooperated fully with the police and answered all of their questions; however, Kate refused to answer the authority's question on advice from her attorney.

On September 10th, 2007, the head of the local police department signed a report which concluded that Madeleine had died accidentally in the McCann's apartment and that the McCanns had faked an abduction in order to hide their role in their daughter's death.

Conclusion

Despite the views of the Portuguese investigators, as well as the information uncovered by Scotland Yard, it is likely that the truth surrounding Madeleine's disappearance may never be fully known. While the McCanns and members of the Tapas Seven were accused of being involved in Madeleine's disappearance several times over the years, they have repeatedly denied any involvement in the abduction. Furthermore, both the McCanns and several members of the Tapas Seven have won libel suits against news organizations who accused them of being involved in Madeleine's disappearance.

BEAUMONT CHILDREN

It was a warm summer morning on January 26, 1966, when the three Beaumont children left their suburban home to celebrate Australia Day at the beach. The children regularly made the trip by themselves, so their mother felt at ease providing them with bus fare and sending them on their way while she visited and had lunch with a close friend. However, she would return home that afternoon to find that the children still had not returned. That morning would end up being the last time she saw her three children.

Jane (aged 9), Arnna (aged 7), and Grant (aged 4), lived in Somerton Park, a quiet suburb minutes away from Adelaide, South Australia. Their father, Jim Beaumont, was a linen goods salesman who frequently traveled for work and their mother, Nancy Beaumont, was a stay-at-home mother.

The oldest child, Jane, was viewed by her parents as responsible enough to supervise the other children for short trips and adventures, a style of parenting that was the norm in Australia at that time. The children frequently took the five-minute bus ride to neighboring Glenely Beach by themselves and were looking forward to celebrating the national holiday at the beach.

The children left their home at 10:00am that morning and were seen arriving at the beach by witnesses at 10:15am. They spent much of that morning at play on the beach and were supposed to arrive home at 2:00pm. When they did not arrive at the appointed time, their mother assumed that they had become preoccupied with celebrating the holiday with their playmates and that they would arrive on the next bus or had decided to walk home, something that the three children had done before. When the children did not disembark from the next scheduled bus, their mother began to grow worried.

The disappearance of the Beaumont children would result in one of the largest manhunts and police investigations in Australian history. Furthermore, the event had widespread consequences on Australian society, shattering the illusion that many parents had regarding their children's safety and changing the way that Australians parented their children forever.

Timeline of Events

10:00am - The children leave their Somerton Park home to travel to Glenely Beach by bus.

10:15am - They are seen exiting the bus by multiple witnesses.

11:00am - The three children are spotted playing beneath a sprinkler by an elderly woman. A tall blond man is spotted lying on the ground next to them, watching the children play.

11:15am - A tall blond man is seen playing with the children. They all appear to be laughing and at ease.

11:45am - The children purchase several pastries and a meat pie from the beach snack shop.

12:15pm - The tall blond man and the children are seen leaving the beach together. The children are witnessed laughing together and holding hands.

3:00pm - A postman on his route spots the children walking along Jetty Road alone, away from the beach. The postman is known to the children and they exchange greetings. Police believe that the timeline for this event is incorrect.

7:20pm - The parents of the children become gravely concerned and file a missing children's report with the local police department. Jim Beaumont and the local police search the entire Glenely Beach area.

8:40pm - Police search the surrounding beaches with

no results. The father contacts friends and relatives in an attempt to locate the children.

10:00pm - Police issue public radio announcements with a missing children report.

Points of Interest

There are several details in this story which raised doubts with both the parents of the children and the local police department. When the children departed for Glenely Beach in the morning of January 26th, they left with only enough money to cover their bus fare: six shilling and a sixpence. However, the shop owner, who sold several pastries and a meat pie to the children at 11:45am, reported that the children paid for the food with a $1 bill, an amount of money that they did not have when they left their mother's care.

In addition, the shop owner knew the children well and had sold them food and pastries several times before. He reported that the children had never purchased a meat pie before. This suggests that the children received the money from someone after leaving their parents home and that they may have been purchasing the meat pie for someone else.

Lastly, the mother of the children, Nancy Beaumont, repeatedly said that her children were quite shy and very unlikely to speak with strangers, indicating that they may have met the tall blond man prior to the date of their disappearance. Their mother also remembered a seemingly innocuous comment from Arnna, who had previously told her mother that Jane had "got a boyfriend down the beach." Nancy assumed that her daughter was referring to a young playmate, but in hindsight it seems that she may have been referring to the tall blond man spotted by witnesses.

Police Investigation

The South Australian police force began investigating the disappearance of the children in full-force the evening of their disappearance. After interviewing several witnesses who were present at Glenely Beach, they were able to determine that the children were playing with a tall blond, "thin-faced" man while at the beach. He was described as being a blond man in his late 30s with a thin or athletic build.

"Things seemed bungled from the get-go," forensic psychologist Paula Orange said. "First off, the artist drawing the picture admitted to being drunk at the time of completing his task. So the sketch made of the suspect looks more like a lantern-jawed alien than a real person. Secondly, the witnesses claimed that the man was in his late thirties. Witnesses are notorious for getting ages wrong and the police dismissed too many possible subjects out of hand because they didn't fit the profile."

Several witnesses stated that the man was seen dressing the children prior to leaving the beach. The children's parents said that the kids, especially Jane, were very shy and unlikely to speak to a stranger. This later led police to theorize that the children had met the man in question prior to the date of their disappearance and had grown to know him over a period of several weeks.

The blond man and three children were seen leaving the beach together at 12:15pm, after the children purchased several pastries and a meat pie from a local vendor with a $1 bill, an amount of money that they did not have when they left their home that morning.

A wrench was thrown into the investigation when a postman, who knew the children and was on friendly terms with them, reported that he saw the children around 3:00pm that afternoon walking away from the beach and in the direction of their home in Somerton Park. He stated that he exchanged greetings with the young children and that they seemed to be in good spirits. In particular, the postman said that he say the children were "holding hands and laughing" as they walked down the road alone, with no blond companion in sight. Police later said that they believed the postman was mistaken about the timeline and that he most likely saw the children walking some time before noon.

Several months later, a woman in a nearby neighborhood contacted police and told them that she had seen a man with two girls and a young boy enter an abandoned house on her street. She also reported seeing the young boy walking away from the house before he was roughly grabbed by, and returned to the house with, the older man. She never saw the man or children again.

"The response from the public was overwhelming," Orange said. "People drove from miles away to aid in the search. They combed the beach and drained part of it all to no avail. They found nothing, not a trace."

The police were quickly able to eliminate drowning as the cause of the children's disappearance as a result of several witnesses saying that they saw the children leave the beach around 12:15pm. Furthermore, all of the children's belongings were missing, lending further support to the theory that they left the beach. After speaking with the parents, the police were able to identify seventeen different items that were carried by the children that day, providing a list of items that could be used to identify their remains or whereabouts. However, the police's continue efforts continued to prove fruitless.

The Psychic Circus

On November 8, 1966, nearly a year after the children's initial disappearance, an internationally-renowned psychic from the Netherlands, Gerard Croiset, was flown to Australia to investigate the case. His presence caused a whirlwind of media coverage in Australia and across the world. After making a series of outlandish and ever-changing claims, Croiset claimed that the children were buried underneath a warehouse just minutes away from the children's school.

"I appreciate him (Gerard Croiset) coming out to find the children," Jim Beaumont said. "But I don't believe what he said. I don't believe the children are dead and will continue to believe until given evidence that proves otherwise."

The building, which was under construction at the time of their disappearance, was eventually razed and excavated after the owners raised $40,000 for the project as a result of public pressure. No evidence of the children or their belongings were ever found.

"The press and police followed Croiset around everywhere," Orange said. "He was an obvious con artist but they were desperate. They had nothing."

A Series of Letters

Beginning in 1968, the parents of the three children began to receive a series of letters which rekindled hope in the idea that their children may still be alive. Postmarked from Dandernong, Victoria, the series of letters claimed to be written by Jane, the eldest daughter. She claimed to be under the supervision of a man and in good health and care, saying

Dear Mum and Dad,

We had a beautiful lunch today...The man is feeding us really well. The man took us to see The Sound of Music yesterday.

Police officers believed the letters to be from Jane after comparing them to examples of her handwriting and, as far as 1981, the Sidney Morning Herald produced analysis from handwriting experts claiming that the letters were actually from the missing child.

Following receipt of the letters supposedly sent from Jane, the parents received a letter from a man claiming to be in possession of the children. He said that he was willing to hand the children over to the parents at a specific time and location. The Beaumonts arrived at the appointed time and location with an undercover police officer but no one showed. They later received a letter from the same man claiming that he saw the undercover police officer arrive with the parents and that he would now keep the children, ending any hope of a peaceful exchange.

In 1992, following another investigation and remarkable achievements in fingerprint technology, authorities identified the author of the letters as a local man who was just a teenager at the time of the hoax. He reportedly wrote and mailed the letters as "a joke."

False Closure

Then, in November 2013, South Australian police received an anonymous tip claiming that the children were buried underneath a warehouse located in North Plympton. Although radar identified "one small anomaly, which can indicate movement or objects within the soil," no evidence was ever found.

The Suspects

Bevan Spencer von Einem

Bevan Spencer von Einem has long been considered the prime suspect in the disappearance of the Beaumont children. Einem was convicted of the July 1983 murder of fifteen-year-old Richard Kelvin, son of a popular news reporter, in 1984. Police have long suspected Einem of working with a series of accomplices and of having committed other abductions and murders.

In 1983, a police informant known as "Mr. B" told police that Einem claimed to have taken three children from a beach to perform medical "experiments," claiming that he performed "brilliant surgery" on the three children before accidentally killing one of them. Following the child's accidental death, the informant stated that Einem claimed to have killed the other two children and buried them in an open field outside the city of Adelaide.

Einem did bare some resemblance to the descriptions of the tall blond man given to police following the disappearance of the Beaumont children and was known to frequent Glenely Beach to spy on people in the changing rooms. He was also noted as having an obsession with children.

Einem worked as an accountant and lived with his mother. There were rumors that he was part of a ring of Adelaide professionals who shared a "hobby" of kidnapping, drugging and raping boys.

"Einem did match the description of the police sketches," Orange said. "And he did like to frequent the same beach. He seemed more interested in young teenage males as his list of known victims would indicate. Einem was a homosexual who picked up hitchhikers with his transvestite friend where they would engage in a "rough trade" style of sex. He would take photographs of his victims as a keepsake. The three young children would seem to be outside of his modus operandi."

However, Einem was significantly younger than the suspect described by witnesses; Einem was around 20 years old at the time, while the description of the suspect placed him in his late 20s. But, in 2007 local police officers identified a young man who looked exactly like a young Einem in Channel 7 news footage of the incident taken days after the disappearance. He remains a prime suspect in the case.

"The newly found news footage does implicate Einem in a psychological way," Orange said. "Killers often like to return to the scene of the crime. He was spotted on film, days after the disappearance. What are the odds against that?"

Arthur Stanley Brown

Arthur Stanley Brown, along with Einem, is considered to be one of two prime suspects in the abduction of the Beaumont children. In 1988, Brown, then 86 years old, was charged with kidnapping, raping, and murdering Judith and Susan Mackey in Townsville, Queensland. His first trial was declared a mistrial after the jury failed to reach a verdict in the case and his second trial was blocked because he was declared unfit to stand trial; Brown was suffering from dementia and Alzheimer's disease by this time.

He is considered one of two prime suspects in the case because of his connection to the murder of other children and because of his remarkable resemblance to descriptions of the tall blond man seen with the children at the time of their disappearance. He was also a prime suspect in the Adelaide Oval case, which involved the disappearance of Joanna Ratcliffe and Kirste Gordon.

"Brown was a known pedophile by his closest family members," Orange said. "He is alleged to have molested numerous younger relatives. He could be placed in the same area and time of the Beaumont children but nothing could be proven."

Although Brown is considered to be a prime suspect in the disappearance of the Beaumont children, the suspect in the case was identified as being in his late

30s; Brown was in his 50s at the time. Brown died in 2002 without ever admitting to the crime.

"Brown would move into a nursing home at the end of his life," Orange said. "He would die an innocent man with the courts never able to officially charge him because of his Alzheimer's."

James Ryan O'Neill

James Ryan O'Neill, convicted of murdering nine-year-old Ricky John Smith in the Australian state of Tasmania in 1975 and currently serving a life sentence for the crime, was considered as a suspect in the Beaumont children disappearance for some time. He is reported as having told several friends in the early 1970s that he was responsible for the disappearance of the Beaumont children in 1966. However, he was publicly eliminated as a suspect by the South Australian police. He remains in prison in Tasmania to this day.

"O'Neill was the subject of a documentary called 'The Fishermen'," Orange said. "In the documentary, he is evasive about being the man behind the disappearance of the children. He is, however, at the forefront of most pundits who have studied the story. While Brown and Einem did not have charming personas, O'Neill did. He was handsome and smiley with the ability to manipulate everyone around him. He could fabricate lies at the drop of a hat so it is easy to believe that he would be able to charm the children into his acquaintance. People who knew him all described him as 'the most likable man you'll ever meet.' No one could believe that he would be capable of such an act."

Derek Ernest Percy

In 2007, the Victorian newspaper The Age published a report stating that Derek Ernest Percy, at the time the longest-serving prisoner in the southeastern Australian state, was responsible for the disappearance of the Beaumont children in 1966. Initially jailed in 1970 for the 1969 murder of 12-year-old Yvonne Tuohy, Percy was found not guilty of the crime by reason of insanity, but was nonetheless jailed "indefinitely."

He is widely considered to be Australia's worst child serial killer and is suspected of the killings of the Beaumont children, as well as the abduction, attempted rape, and stabbing of Marianne Schmidt and Christine Sharrock on January 11, 1965. In October 2014, Percy was also ruled to have abducted and killed seven-year-old Linda Stilwell in 1968. However, Percy passed away from cancer in 2013, having never admitted to any of his crimes. He remains a possible suspect in the case.

"Percy is unique in that he may have had his mother not aiding him but covering up for him," Orange said. "He is certainly one of the most sadistic pedophiles on record, his doings are unmentionable out of respect for his victims. He was in the city at the time of the Beaumont children disappearance and is probably the top suspect along with O'Neill. His mother, however, has thrown out a lot of what could have been evidence in the case."

Related Cases

Two similar cases to the disappearance of the Beaumont children attracted widespread attention in the South Australian media, and the primary suspect in the Beaumont children's kidnapping case was convicted in one case and suspected in the other.

The Adelaide Oval Case

On August 25, 1972, two young girls, Joanne Ratcliffe

(aged 11) and Kirste Gordon (aged 4) went missing while attending an Australian football game. They are presumed dead. This case also received widespread attention in the South Australian media and Bevan Spencer von Einem was considered the primary suspect in their disappearance.

Einem matched the descriptions of the tall blond man provided by witnesses in the Beaumont children's case and closely resembles the police sketch released to the public. A private police report in leaked in 1989 identified Einem as the primary suspect in the case.

The Family Murders

From 1973 to 1983, a group of men is believed to have been involved in the abduction, rape, and murder of a series of young men and male teenagers in the Adelaide area. Five teens were killed during this time period, including Alan Barnes (aged 16), Neil Muir (aged 25), Peter Stogneff (aged 14), Mark Langley (aged 18), and Richard Kelvin (aged 15). All victims were abducted and subjected to extended bouts of torture and physical assault, including sexual assault and medical experimentation.

Bevan Spencer von Einem was convicted of the

abduction and murder of Richard Kelvin 1984 and is currently serving life in prison in Port Augusta prison. In 1990, he was also charged with the murder of Alan Barnes and Mark Langley, but key evidence from the Richard Kelvin murder was ruled inadmissible in the trial. Following the ruling against this key evidence, the prosecution dropped these charges against Einem on December 21, 1990.

Although Einem was the only member of this group to be convicted, and four out of five of The Family Murders remain unsolved, law enforcement officials believe that Einem was part of a white-collar group that preyed on young children. He remains the prime, and only living, suspect in the disappearance of the Beaumont children.

Impact on the Parents

Jim and Nancy Beaumont continued to hold out hope of finding their children for several decades after their disappearance. In fact, the couple continued to live at the Somerton Park home, at 109 Harding Street, that they shared with their children for nearly two decades, hoping that the children would return home someday. Nancy Beaumont was reported as saying that it would be "dreadful" if the children returned to the home only to find that their parents had moved.

"The Beaumonts left the rooms of the children untouched," Orange said. "Every toy, every book even the bed was left exactly as the children had left them."

The couple were never considered as suspects in the case and cooperated with the police at every turn in the investigation, including working with the police and searching in vain every time a new lead developed in the case over the next several decades.

According to The Age, the parents "have since separated, but still live in Adelaide." The stress and sorrow that resulted from their children's abduction, combined with the constant new leads and media attention is said to have contributed to the failure of their marriage.

Jim, in particular, is said to still be suffering from intense and inconsolable grief every time a new development is reported. Nancy was also reported to have suffered extreme grief and horror when, in 1990, several Australian newspapers released computer-generated images of what her children would look like after aging several decades. She reportedly refused to look at the pictures.

"Jim was a little bit stronger than Nancy," Orange said. "He would address the media more than she did. But they both suffered terribly for the rest of their lives into their eighties. They would spend over fifty years wishing for their children's return, getting false hope after false hope, one false lead after another which would all ultimately turn up nothing. It was a horrific cruelty."

Lastly, Jim and Nancy have largely been seen as sympathetic and pitiable figures in the Australian media and in society at large. Although their actions may seem reckless or irresponsible by today's standards, Australian society was viewed as extremely safe in the 1960s and their policy of allowing a child to supervise their younger siblings both in the home and in public was practiced by a large portion of Australian parents.

Impact on Australian Society

The disappearance of the Beaumont children became an overnight sensation in Australia, led to one of the largest police searches in the country's history, and remains the most famous missing persons case in the country. Prior to this incident, Australia was largely viewed as one of the safest societies on the planet and children were allowed to roam freely, doors remained unlocked at all times, and there was little fear of strangers. All of that changed overnight.

"Australia lost its innocence with the disappearance of the Beaumont Children," Orange said. "For three young children to disappear was unheard of. The city where they grew up was a dignified place, a safe place. But it was all an illusion that went away the day the children went missing."

During the initial search for the children, Jim Beaumont went on national television to appeal for their safe return. His heartfelt address to the nation had a lasting impact on the parents and children who watched his plea. Hundreds of viewers called into the station to offer tips and Australian police report that hundreds of tips continue to come in every year to this day. His image on national television continues to serve as a warning for those who believe in the incorruptibility of their fellow citizens and in the safety of their country.

"A lot of people today will blame the parents for letting them go on the bus alone," Adelaide resident Rachel Harding said. "But times were different back then. Back then kids would walk to school by themselves. Kids were told not to talk to strangers. The Beaumonts did tell their children to not talk to children. But child molesters are cunning monsters. My guess is that he may have stolen the eldest child's purse then conned them into seeing him as their benefactor. They would not have had money to get home then along comes this "blonde man" who offers them money. Buys them food and promises to take them home."

Children who came of age in Australia during the 1960s have remarked that there was a definite culture shift following the Beaumont children's disappearance, often describing a "before" and "after." While children were once allowed to roam freely and interact with strangers, Australian parents have since altered their style of parenting and curtailed the amount of freedom offered to young children.

"It was the type of case where we believe there was a lone offender," Australian police detective Des Bray said. "It isn't the type of crime where one would go around bragging about. But we do hope that he told someone and that somebody knows something."

If the Beaumont children are alive today, they would all be in their 50s and would have lived through years of hearing their names and story broadcast on national television and reported on breathlessly in national newspapers. Despite the vast amount of information we have on the case, their fates may never be known with any certainty.

Both Jim and Nancy Beaumont are still alive, and as of this writing they are ninety and eighty-years old respectively. The anonymous tips and false hopes continue to come in today as they did over fifty years ago.

THE STRANGE DISAPPEARANCE OF PATRICIA MEEHAN

NATHAN NIXON

Patricia Meehan Disappearance

The story of Patricia Meehan is a very strange and puzzling one. She seemingly disappeared into the night with little reason. The case has remained unsolved since 1989. With few witnesses, the full events are sketchy at best. What is well known about this case is that our culture has seemingly thought of every possible scenario to explain what happened to her. To understand and possibly solve the case, understanding the person that Patricia Meehan was is of paramount importance.

Patricia Meehan was never afraid of change. Her path of life took her all over the United States and to nearly every type of region. She was born on November 1, 1951 in Pittsburgh, Pennsylvania. She lived a typical life. She was said to have been "the perfect child" by her loving parents and by all who knew her. She had great ambition to see the world and to attack life with a smile. Socially she was on the same level as her peers. When she decided to attend college in Oklahoma City, Oklahoma, no one was really surprised. That was who Patricia was. That is exactly what she did.

She studied early childhood development and earned her degree in four years of college study. Again, she was living the American dream and successfully setting up a future to thrive. She made many friends in Oklahoma, even though it was a foreign place to a young woman from Pittsburgh. She took up a career in early childhood caregiving in Oklahoma and thrived in the profession for nearly 10 years. She was unhappy, or perhaps, unfulfilled in her work. She sporadically spoke with her family and a few friends from back home in Pennsylvania at the time. People knew Patricia to take risks. She was never afraid to change her outlook if it meant a new adventure or perhaps a new challenge lay ahead. In 1985, she made a major life change that would, effectively, lead to her ultimate disappearance.

She had informed her parents in the years prior that she wanted to become involved in animal care. She made this a reality when she moved to Bozeman, Montana in 1985. She moved alone. Patricia was not married and had left her simple, safe life behind in Oklahoma to pursue a career as a ranch hand. While this major career shift was motivated to start a happier life, it ultimately didn't always pay the bills. She worked numerous odd-jobs in the industry and could successfully make ends meet on her own. She continued this new lifestyle for four years in Bozeman, Montana.

The last person that can be fully confirmed to have seen Patricia Meehan alive was her landlord. Meehan's landlord reported to police investigators later that she seemed much more hyper than normal. This struck the landlord as extremely odd for the normally mellow, collected Patricia. Nonetheless, there were absolutely no problems between the two in any way. Patricia always paid her rent and was an "overall great tenant" to have.

The evening of April 20, 1989 is one of great speculation as to what really happened. The testimony of Peggy Bueller has always been a key component to the theories of Patricia's disappearance.

At approximately 8:05 P.M. Peggy Bueller and her father were traveling west bound on Montana State Highway 200. They were passing through the tiny town of Circle, Montana. To their surprise, they could see a set of vehicle headlights heading straight at them up ahead. A vehicle heading east was driving on the wrong side of the road. Peggy managed to swerve onto the shoulder and avoid a head-on collision with the opposing driver. The car that had been following behind Peggy was driven by an off-duty police dispatcher named Carol Heitz. Unfortunately for Carol, she was not able to swerve and avoid a collision.

Peggy Bueller had pulled over and gazed in her rear-view mirror in time to see the collision with the car driven by Carol Heitz. Thankfully, no injuries occurred in the accident. The story is very odd and somewhat eerie from this point. Just after impact, Carol Heitz emerged from her vehicle unharmed. She was shook up, but suffered no major injury. Being a police dispatcher, her first concern was for the other driver. The car that was traveling east bound was driven by Patricia Meehan. Patricia was next to emerge from her car after the impact. She stood in the middle of the road, and proceeded to slowly approach the car of Carol

Heitz. According to Heitz, Patricia Meehan did not utter a single word. "She approached me calmly and silently," Heitz reported. "She seemingly stared directly through me from the moment she began to approach me."

Peggy Bueller remained in her vehicle and observed what was taking place. What she observed was "one of the strangest acts" she had ever seen. Peggy and Heitz agree that Patricia climbed over a fence just off of the road after she passed by Carol. She took only a step after getting over the fence and turned back around to stare upon the accident. She made no noise or any sort of expression. She stood there for at least two minutes. Heitz described Meehan as someone who seemed to be observing the accident scene rather than someone who had been involved in the accident. After a few short minutes, Meehan turned around and walked into a secluded Montana field into the pitch dark night. This was the last confirmed sighting of Patricia Meehan. By the time police arrived to sort out the accident, the whereabouts of Patricia were unknown. Peggy and Carol gave the exact same story in separate interviews with investigators. As eerie as the accident had unfolded, it had ended quietly and abruptly. Patricia Meehan was officially gone.

Peggy Bueller quickly drove into town when Patricia disappeared into the night. Her father stayed with Carol Heitz at the scene of the accident. Peggy reached a phone within ten minutes and alerted the authorities. When police arrived, an extensive search of the field where Patricia was seen walking away to turned up nothing. It only took police 15 minutes to identify the then mystery woman as Patricia Meehan after they ran the license plate of the vehicle. She was a registered member of the Bozeman, Montana community and had no criminal record. This was shocking to police who had assumed the woman left due to the fact that police would be arriving to the scene to investigate the accident. This posed the burning question that is still unanswered of why this woman would leave the scene of the accident if she had no criminal record.

Police made efforts to investigate the field immediately following the accident. Police discovered a tennis shoe about a mile into the field that had been accompanying a trail of footprints. The shoe matched what would have been the approximate size of the foot of Patricia Meehan. Oddly enough, the tracks seemingly disappear. Due to darkness, the investigation was suspended until the following morning of April 21. When police arrived to further check for a trail, the footprints led to nothing. The terrain had an influence in this as well as the fact that the actual shoe prints were gone, likely due to Patricia going barefoot at this point in her walk. Police had no leads.

There were two major theories that investigators had arrived at to this point. The first was the most likely. They believed that Patricia had hitchhiked from a small rural road in the area with a trucker. This could obviously not be confirmed, however the lack of a body, further clothes or footprints, as well as a lack of any whereabouts in surrounding cities points to this to be the likely case. The second theory they had suggest that she stowed away in a hay truck in the area and accomplished the same thing. This proved later to be unlikely as no hay trucks were confirmed to be in the field or in the immediate area.

The Meehan family arrived to Montana from Pittsburgh in the day following the accident. They distributed over 2,000 missing person flyers in the surrounding Montana towns and provided police with valuable information. The flyers turned up numerous calls, however none of these would lead to finding Patricia. Over 500 local volunteers searched the mountainous terrain around the accident site in an effort to possibly locate Patricia. For days, people walked the area. Some even brought dogs to perhaps catch a scent trail. These searches turned up absolutely nothing. There was no evidence of human activity in the mountains, and there were no evidence of a body or struggle in the surrounding area. Patricia had seemingly disappeared without a trace after taking a path into a secluded field. Perhaps the events in the days and weeks prior could shed some light into who Patricia was and things she had been recently going through.

The Meehan family revealed to police that Patricia had been going through some dark times in the past couple of months. Patricia was somewhat at a dead end and was feeling lost. She had asked her parents if she could return home in an effort to get back on track. Her parent's agreed, but only if she see a psychologist leading to coming home. Patricia agreed. She was diagnosed as suffering from depression. Ironically, she had an appointment with her psychologist the morning after the accident on April 21. She obviously never made this appointment.

Police also were suspicious as to why Patricia was even in this part of the state anyway. She had an appointment in Bozeman, Montana for the next morning. Bozeman was where she was living. The direction of travel she was taking at the time of the accident was in the opposite direction of Bozeman. Investigators asked the Meehan family if they had any idea where she may be going or what she was doing in this remote part of Montana. They had absolutely no idea. It was evident to police that she had no intention of returning to Bozeman to make her appointment the next morning. But could there be more to this part of the story?

The Meehan family had a roll of film developed that had been found in Patricia's car the night of the accident. The film was fully used. There were numerous pictures of nature. Beautiful countryside and the secluded area that Patricia loved. There were also numerous pictures of animals, specifically horses, that Patricia had devoted her life to in the recent years. Patricia's family stumbled across one picture that was quite alarming. A random picture that Patricia had taken in front of a mirror. She had a very confused look on her face and seemed lost. Investigation of the picture by mental professionals led some to believe she could have been suffering from amnesia. This could obviously not be proven, but would go further in explaining the odd behavior she displayed that night. Some of the investigators pointed to this as a possible reason that she was driving away from Bozeman and was 300 miles away from home. Could she simply have forgotten how to get home? Could her mental health had gotten that bad?

Patricia had been driving on the wrong side of the road and made no effort to swerve. Police drew two possible conclusions to this fact. The first was that she was so far lost in amnesia that she simply didn't think she was doing anything wrong or perhaps forgot the basic rules of driving. The second was that she was possibly trying to harm herself or had gotten so careless that the results were not clearly thought through. These are obviously speculation and will never be proven one way or the other. The mental health of Patricia was most assuredly in a low place.

The roll of film that was developed also proved something else to investigators and the Meehan family. Socially, she was in a dark place also. Out of every picture that had been developed, not one of them featured people that weren't named Patricia Meehan. This is clearly not the norm. Patricia had mentioned that she had had a few boyfriends since arriving in Montana, but nothing serious and committal. She had previously mentioned to her parents that she had become lonely and never really made any friends in her new home. This could help to explain the depression and possible mental health issues that she had developed.

Over the last 25 years, there have been over 5,000 reported sightings of Patricia Meehan. Through all of this, only 3 of those do police feel could be Patricia or are even likely to be her. In the days following her disappearance, there were some interesting leads that were generated by the public calls on the missing person flyers.

On May 4, 1989 just two weeks after the accident, a strong lead was generated out of Luverne, Minnesota. Out of all of the possible sightings, this is considered by police and those surrounding the case to be the most likely sighting of Patricia. A police officer in Luverne claimed to have seen Patricia sitting in a Hardee's restaurant by herself. For over five hours, she was sitting in corner booth drinking water. She remained until closing time, and then proceeded to walk to a nearby 24 hour diner. Here, the officer questioned her. The woman refused adamantly to give her name. She first said that she was from Colorado, and later said she was from Israel. The major problem with all of this is that the officer could not detain her. She had done nothing wrong. However, he left without further checking to identify her. This was perhaps the best chance to obtain Patricia if this indeed was her. The officer left and where this mystery woman went next is unknown.

Another interesting sighting occurred on May 19, 1989. This is nearly one full month after the accident. A waitress at a local restaurant in Bozeman, Montana reported seeing Patricia eating there. She informed police that Patricia at in a hurry and said she had to go shopping at 9 A.M. She said she was polite, but did seem to be displaying odd behavior. Another waitress on the same shift also reported seeing her. This waitress said she was talking to herself and seemed disoriented. Patricia left the restaurant and again, no attempts were really made to investigate who she really was.

The theories that surround this case are perhaps the most interesting in the current media. If Patricia was alive today, she would be in her late 60's. This would obviously make her hard to identify in the general public. This leads to the first theory.

The first, and generally most believed theory, is that Patricia simply wanted another fresh start. She had done this in the past, albeit in a much less drastic way. She wanted a fresh start after high school, so she attended college in Oklahoma City, Oklahoma. She wanted a career change and a change of passion nearly 10 years after she started her career, so she moved to Bozeman, Montana and became a ranch hand. Many feel that she again wanted a career change and a life change at this point in her life. Turning to her parents, they gave her an ultimatum to see a psychologist before she came home. The theory suggest that she wasn't happy with her family about this. She obtained her fresh start by planning an event that would allow her to vanish into the unknown. What better place to accomplish this than a secluded highway in rural Montana where she could simply walk away.

This theory goes on further to explain that she had walked across the field and met up with someone who would drive her away. This theory doesn't sound too crazy at this juncture. The who or why is unknown, but the basis of the theory is mostly sound. Where she would have started this new life is completely unknown. But for a person who was struggling socially, not completely happy, and perhaps not enjoying the rural life as much as she had anticipated, this theory makes some sense.

The second popular theory is the more logical, medically supported theory. The collision that Patricia Meehan had was significant. While there were no injuries on the exterior, a concussion is without a doubt a possibility of this type of vehicle accident. Some believe that it was not amnesia to blame, but a concussion that would cause her to act so disoriented after the accident. The theory suggest that she exited her vehicle with a head injury and collapsed in the field shortly after beginning her walk into the night.

Montana is home to vast amounts of wildlife and has a very abstract climate. The night time temperatures in April in Montana typically are going to approach freezing. Anything under 50 degrees at altitude is going to be a severe situation for a minimally clothed, small woman with a possible head injury. The theory suggest that she was unconscious overnight and perhaps was eaten by animals, which would explain the lack of a body or any other evidence to her disappearance. It is for this reason that the theory is typically not accepted. Even with this, there would have been signs of this happening by one of the numerous volunteers or investigators in the following days.

    The disappearance of Patricia Meehan has garnered national attention for the past 25 years. On November 1, 1989 the case was featured on *Unsolved Mysteries*. This would have marked the 38th birthday for Patricia.

    Sightings are still reported on Patricia and a host of other in the United States. With each passing year, it is all too assuring that this case will never be solved. The lack of information on the case is puzzling. Those who choose to research the case will find that there is little information beyond the night of the accident and some significant reported sightings. All of these factors have led to a disappearance that has stumped police since that fateful night.

    Patricia Meehan was an ambitious woman. She took risk in efforts to accomplish her goals and to get the most out of life. Anyone who ever knew her would say that she was a wonderful person with a positive view of the world. She loved her family dearly, and she loved her life deeply. She confidently left home to discover new opportunities on multiple occasions. It seems that life perhaps got too much for her in Montana. Maybe she just wanted to come home. Whatever the case, Patricia Meehan disappeared in April 1989, and has yet to be found. This beautiful young woman hasn't officially turned up in over 25 years. This tragic case may never be closed. A sure fact of the case is that Patricia was a sweet woman who didn't get in this situation by means of risky behavior or negative interactions. Likely, her disappearance can be attributed to a social low spot where she needed help that she didn't go through with getting. Maybe one day the truth of where her walk ultimately led will come out.

ARLIS PERRY

    Arlis Kay Perry was a newly married nineteen-year-old when she entered Stanford Memorial Church at Stanford University in the late night hours of October 12th, 1974. She would be found the next morning, the victim of a brutal murder in what appeared to be a ritualistic killing.

    Her case has remained unsolved for the past

forty-two years. Various rumors and theories abound as to who her murderer was. There is conjecture that she was the victim of the Son of Sam, the Zodiac Killer, the Death Angels and the Process Church.

The police never obtained solid leads on her case and it remains as much a mystery today as it was over forty years ago.

Who killed Arlis Perry?

EARLY LIFE

Arlis was born on February 22nd, 1955 in Linton, North Dakota to Marvin Dykema and Jean Van Beek. She usually wore glasses and had her hair straight. In the lone picture of her available online, her hair is wavy and she is not wearing glasses. This is an unfamiliar look for her and no one knows where or when the picture was taken. She was small, at 5'6" and weighing 110 lbs.

Arlis would graduate from Bismarck High School in 1973 where she was a cheerleader and a member of the Fellowship of Christian Athletes. She had a high school sweetheart, Bruce Perry, and they were both born again Christians. Bruce would be accepted into Stanford University upon graduation while Arlis would stay behind in Bismarck. She remained active in her church as a Sunday school teacher in the Bismarck reformed church.

Then she came into contact with people from the Process Church.

They were six young men that were renting a home across the street from her grandmother. Their names were Father Christian, Brother Thomas, Brother Joseph and three other men who were called "initiates."

The men tried to initiate Arlis into their religion but she soon became disenchanted with their belief system.

She realized that the were devil worshipers.

Arlis then made it a point to try and proselytize anyone who was involved in their church, leading them from Satanism into Christianity.

THE PROCESS CHURCH

The Process Cult became controversial in the early 1970s with its strong ties to the Manson family. Their belief system allowed them to worship both Christ and Satan. The church started in both Los Angeles and New York but branched out to North Dakota, as its leaders wanted the isolation of the hills and woods.

They would have meetings at the Hillside Cemetery in Bismarck and a wooded area behind Mary College. It was here that they would steal the dogs of people who lived in a nearby trailer park and sacrifice them in satanic rituals. People were complaining that they would find their dogs lying dead inside a "majick circle", their bodies badly mutilated.

MOVING TO CALIFORNIA

After graduation, Arlis would continue to participate in the Fellowship of Christian Athletes as a "huddle leader" as well as taking a job as a receptionist in a dental office. She would attend the local junior college for a year as she corresponded with Bruce Perry who was in his first year of studies at Stanford.

Bruce would return home and ask for Arlis' hand in marriage. She would accept and join him as he returned for his second year in Stanford's pre-med program.

Bruce's studies did not leave a lot of time for Arlis and she became a bit restless. She would take a job as a receptionist at a law firm to occupy her time during the day when Bruce would be away, finding work at the law firm Spaeth, Blase, Valentine, and Klein in Palo Alto.

The couple lived at the Quillen House in Escondido Village which was a campus housing unit for married couples.

Arlis got into the habit of taking nightly walks around the campus. Bruce worried for her safety and advised her not to. She stopped the practice until one night she wanted to get out of the home and mail off some letters.

DEADLY CHURCH VISIT

On October 12th, 1974 at around 11: 30 pm, Bruce and Arlis were walking on the Stanford campus. They would discover that the tire on Arlis' car had gone flat. They would have a minor argument as to who was going to take care of it. Bruce went back to the dorm and Arlis would go to the Memorial Church, telling Bruce that she wanted to pray alone.

Arlis entered and several people remembered seeing her. A security guard told her that it was almost midnight and the church was about the close up. She remained inside, however, and witnesses remembered seeing a "sandy-haired man" walk inside.

Arlis didn't return home after several hours and Bruce went out to look for her.

When he didn't find her, he called the police.

The next morning at around 05:45 am, security guard Steve Crawford would discover her body inside the church.

In Maury Terry's book, "Ultimate Evil", he described Perry's murder scene as follows:

"She was found lying on her back, with her body partially under the first pew on the left side of the alcove, a short distance from where she had been seen praying. Above her was a large carving which had been sculptured into the church wall years before. It was an engraving of the cross. The symbolism was explicit.

Arlis's head was facing forward, toward the main altar. Her legs were spread wide apart, and she was nude from the waist down. The legs of her blue jeans were placed upside down across her calves, purposely arranged in that manner. Viewed from above, the resulting pattern of Arlis's legs and the inverted blue jeans took on a diamond-like shape.

Arlis's blouse was torn open, and her arms were folded across her chest. Placed neatly between her breasts was an altar candle. Completing the desecration, another candle, thirty inches long, was jammed into her vagina. She had been beaten and choked. Death was due to her an ice pick being rammed into her skull behind her left ear, the handle protruding grotesquely from her head."

THE AFTERMATH

Security guard Crawford stated that he had locked up the church a little after midnight. He rechecked that the doors were still locked at around 02:00 a.m.

At 03:00 a.m. Perry had called the police and informed them that his wife was missing. The Santa Clara County Sheriff's went to the church and found all of the doors locked. Crawford would return to the church at 05:45 to unlock the doors and he found the west side door open.

The obvious suspect was Bruce Perry and police immediately went to brutally interrogate him.

"You knew your wife was having an affair so you killed her!"

Perry adamantly denied the questions. The police gave him a polygraph test which he passed.

Investigators would found two pieces of identifying evidence from the scene. They were able to collect a DNA sample which was found in semen near the body. The second was a bloody palm print found on one of the candles.

"It's a typical-if there is such a thing-sexual psychopathic slaying," Santa Clara County Undersheriff Tom Rosa said.

Rumors began to circulate around the campus.

Some people were saying that Arlis was the victim of a satanist torture rite called the "Black Mass."

Rosa disputed the claim.

"It has no cult-like overtones," Rosa said. "It just happened to occur in a church."

There were no signs of a struggle. The detectives believed that Arlis was the victim of a "fast and sudden attack" as she entered the church around midnight.

Bruce would tell authorities that she often went there to pray when she was having problems.

SON OF SAM

Conspiracy theories would abound as the murder would go unsolved for many years. Some believe that Arlis was not murdered by a lone psychopath but by a satanic cult who stalked her from Bismarck, North Dakota.

Because of the way Arlis' body was positioned (legs spread with a candlestick in her breasts and vagina) people familiar with occult activity assumed that this was a ritualistic killing.

Fueling the speculation was some cryptic correspondence from David Berkowitz.

Berkowitz, the "Son of Sam" killer from New York City, had mentioned the Perry killing as he wrote authorities in North Dakota. He said that he had information on the killer, a man he referred to as "Manson II."

In 1979, five years after the murder, Berkowitz would send police authorities in North Dakota a book. In the margin, he had written: "Arlis Perry, hunted, stalked and slain, followed to California, Stanford Univ."

Berkowitz would claim that he was not the only person involved in the string of New York murders, hinting that he was part of a larger Satanic cult.

Detectives would later interview Berkowitz regarding Perry's murder but realized that he had "nothing of value to offer."

Those following the case, however, believe that Berkowitz should have been interrogated harder.

"Why would he make it up? He had no motive, no reason," crime writer Maury Terry asked. "He's confessed to three murders, he's not getting out."

The "Manson II" Berkowitz referred to was William Mentzer. Mentzer was suspected of being the head of the Son of Sam cult, had ties to the Manson family (although not to Charles Manson himself) and was suspected of being the Zodiac killer.

But was he responsible for killing Arlis Perry?

The answer may lie in the fact that at some point Mentzer was involved in a "hit squad" involving the Process Church. He allegedly performed assassin duties for the higher-ups who needed someone killed.

Interestingly, the serial murders of the Zodiac Killer stopped after Mentzer was in prison There were numerous parallels between the Zodiac Killer and Mentzer. Detectives believe that the Zodiac had military training. Mentzer had served in the Marines during Vietnam and killed ten people. Upon his return from the Vietnam War, the killings began in December of 1968.

The Zodiac would stab two of his victims with a

bayonet style knife with rivets. Mentzer had a job where he was making rivets at a local aerospace company.

 The Zodiac killer than began taunting the newspapers, sending them a diagram of a bomb while threatening to blow up a school bus. Mentzer later had a job driving a bus. He also had military training in demolition and plastic explosives. One of the survivors said that the killer spoke in a slow monotone with a drawl. Mentzer speaks the same way.

 After a final letter to the press, the Zodiac mysteriously vanished in 1974.

 Menzer would later be arrested for his role in the brutal murders of Roy Radin in 1983 and a prostitute/ madam named June Mincher in 1984.

 Radin had been shot more than twenty times in the head. Menzer would then put a stick of dynamite in Radin's mouth and blow off his face.

 In the end, however, police didn't believe Menzer had probable cause to be the Zodiac killer and he would never be questioned for the death of Arlis Perry despite the rumors.

 Crime writer Terry would investigate Perry's murder on his own and retrace her steps. He thinks that as many as four people were responsible for her death. He believes that the "sandy-haired" man who visited Perry at the law firm was a cult member from Bismarck, someone that she knew from the Process Church.

 "She (Arlis) might have heard or seen something

she shouldn't have," he said. "They may have feared she would expose them. Someone in Bismarck OK'd this, and someone had the hooks to get help on the West Coast," he said. "This was a pretty sophisticated operation."

BRUCE PERRY

Bruce Perry would complete go on to become a researcher in children's mental health and the neurosciences, becoming an internationally recognized authority in his field.

At Arlis's funeral, one of her law firm co-workers was confused when he saw Bruce. He thought her husband was a different man who had come into the workplace earlier. He witnessed her get into a "heated argument" with the man and assumed it was her husband. The co-worker described this man as "sandy-haired' which would fit the description of the man seen following Arlis into the church the night she was murdered.

Arlis would also note that there were two Bruce Perrys listed in the phone book. There is some speculation that Mentzer pretended to be Bruce Perry and had his name listed in the phone book. People from North Dakota would call and get him instead of Arlis' husband. He would then be able to finagle her whereabouts but subtly asking the family member the right questions.

This is one of the more far-fetched theories. It doesn't seem plausible that Menzer would go to the lengths of putting out a fake name and phone number just to coax Arlis' family and friends to call. Furthermore, he was a black-haired, mustachioed man who did not fit the "sandy-haired" man description.

But what is curious is that Perry's killing would be another instance of a series of unsolved murders that took place in and around the Stanford campus in the early 1970s.

A SERIAL KILLER AT WORK?

The murder of Arlis would be the fourth homicide on the Stanford campus in less than two years as well as the third incident in which the victim was a young woman out alone.

None of the murders were ever solved.

The killings started with Leslie Marie Perlov, a 21-year old Stanford history graduate who worked as a Palo Alto law librarian. She was found strangled to death on February 16th, 1973 in the foothills behind the campus. She had disappeared after leaving her workplace three days earlier.

Perlov's body would be found in a wooded gully where she had a scarf that was "wrapped tightly around her throat." There was no sign of a struggle where her body was found leading authorities to believe she walked there on her own volition.

She was not sexually assaulted but her skirt had been pulled up around her waist and her pantyhose had been stuffed into her mouth. While officers were searching for Perlov, they would find the body of Mark Rosvold, a twenty-five-year-old man out of Palo Alto. Rosvold was believed to have committed suicide the morning after Perlov was murdered. Perlov was last seen near the quarry gate of the Stanford campus, talking to a man with long blonde hair.

Seven months after the Perlov murder, physics student David S. Levine would be found stabbed to death on a walkway just east of the Meyer Undergraduate Library. The attack was estimated to have occurred between 1 and 3 a.m.
An early morning jogger would find the body of Levine. The young man had been stabbed fifteen times in the back and the side.
Like the rest of the murders, there had been no sign of struggle. The detectives believed that the young man was taken by surprise. Levine's empty wallet remained in his pants pocket and they ruled out robbery as a motive for the murder.
Levine was a straight-A student and called brilliant by his fellow students.
San Francisco Mayor Joseph Alioto believed that the murders were the work of a cult called the "Death Angels" who were suspects in the "Zebra" killings in San Francisco. Three months after the murder of Levine, a slaying took place on the UC Berkeley campus that was also rumored to be the work of the "Death Angels."
The Death Angels were a genocidal Black Muslim faction who mostly killed white people from October 1973 to April 1974. They were compromised of four black men: Manuel Moore, Larry Green, Jessie Lee Cooks, J.C.X Simon. The group committed at least

15 murders according to Wikipedia. Author Clark Howard estimates the group to be responsible for as many as two-hundred seventy deaths.

The Death Angeles would use .32 caliber pistols to shoot their victims point blank, however. They would take people by surprise but there were not any instances where they used strangulation or a knife for the initial attack as was the case for Perlov and Levin.

On March 24th, 1974, Janet Ann Taylor was strangled while hitchhiking to her La Honda home after visiting a friend on the Stanford campus. Her body was found early the next morning in a roadside ditch. Taylor was twenty-one years old and the daughter of former Stanford athletic director, Chuck Taylor.

Detectives would later concede that there were "similarities" between the Perlov and Taylor murders.

Both would be strangled although Taylor would be choked by hand instead of a scarf. Neither were sexually violated.

Both were barefoot when their bodies were found and wearing raincoats. Neither of the purses were on the person when their bodies were found.

"We really don't know who we're looking for," Sheriff's Inspector Rudy Siemssen said after the Taylor killing. "We have no motive. She apparently had no money in her purse, although you could speculate that robbery was a motive. It's a rough one."

WHO KILLED THEM?
None of the unsolved Stanford murders seem to

be connected in terms of the method of killing. But, on the surface, they all were senseless and without motivation.

In the case of Arlis, there is mere speculation because of her conversations with the Bismarck Process Cult. The rumor is that someone from the cult, a leader or ordered assassin, came out to California because she tried to convert their members to Christ.

What is curious about the case is how the body was positioned. Arlis' pants were moved but placed on top of her body. The pants were positioned legs up, across her calves and her legs were spread apart. Her arms were in a crucifix position and the altar candle was shoved in her vagina.

Looking at her body from above, she was positioned in the Mason's symbol of Freemasonry. So this suggests that her murder was the work of someone involved in the Freemason cult or someone who was trying to make it look as if there was Freemason involvement.

It also appeared that Arlis may have known her killer. Her meeting with the "sandy-haired" man at work or the church may have been a scheduled meeting place. She was a devout Christian woman, used to doing the right thing, so it seems a bit odd that she wouldn't obey the security guard when he told her he was closing up the church.

The speculation is that she was meeting someone, probably the "sandy-haired" man. Who he was or how they came to meet is the question of the day. The problem is that the police failed to see the cult link in the killing, with some kind of warped religious undertones. How much of an evangelist was Arlis and who exactly did she speak with at the Process Cult in Bismarck?

The police were never interested in pursuing that line of thought.

There were rumors in Bismarck that well-known people were part of a satanic cult that performed all kinds of grisly rituals at Pioneer Park and the caves behind the University of Mary. One witness reported that they remembered seeing people come into town in priest's outfits. Only they weren't wearing white collars. They were wearing red collars and upside-down cross necklaces.

Jon Martinson, a former psychology professor at Bismarck State College, doesn't buy the theory that Arlis was stalked from Bismarck to California.

"I remember a lot of weird religious stories going on around here in that time," Martinson said. "Like covens dancing under the full moon and rituals taking place down by the river bottoms. But in her case, I think she was at the wrong place at the wrong time."

After Terry's book "The Ultimate Evil" came out, students around the Bismarck around began trolling around the University of Mary looking for any semblance of satanic cult activity. They found none but it became an urban legend around the town. The caves behind the University of Mary were eventually filled in.

Terry still firmly believes that Berkowitz knew

something that the police didn't follow-up on. "It's very important to know that it was Berkowitz himself who raised the connection to (the University of) Mary, and he did it in late 1979 – nearly eight years before The Ultimate Evil was published," Terry said. "Nothing about the Mary (University of Mary) ties to Arlis' death was made public until the book came out. But Berkowitz knew about cult activities there all along. And I also confirmed that rituals had been occurring there in the 1970s."

Ken Kahn was one of the detectives who flew into Attica State Prison in New York to interview Berkowitz. The Son of Sam killer remained vague and didn't fess up to any details. This led Kahn to believe that Berkowitz was simply messing with the crime writer and knew nothing of the murder of Perry or anyone else at Stanford.

Martinson and Terry remain adamant that Berkowitz knows something as he was documented to have been in nearby Minot Air Force base before he committed his own murders. Martinson showed Berkowitz a series of photographs from people who Terry believed was involved with Perry's murder. Berkowitz identified one of the men in the photo as someone he had met during his satanic cult meetings in Minot.

FOREVER COLD

Detectives were hoping that with advanced DNA technology and handprint databases they would get a lead on the who left behind the semen and bloody handprint.

To date, there are still no leads.

Arlis' parents would stay in contact with the Santa Clara Sheriff's Department for more than thirty years.

Eventually, however, the sheriffs would stop returning their calls.

Arlis Perry's murder remains unsolved.

Made in the USA
Monee, IL
08 December 2020